on
deception

Harry Houdini
on
deception

'on'

'on'
Published by Hesperus Press Limited
19 Bulstrode Street, London W1U 2JN
www.hesperuspress.com

First published 1906–20
This collection first published by Hesperus Press Limited, 2009
This edition printed 2011

Foreword © Derren Brown, 2009

Designed and typeset by Fraser Muggeridge studio
Printed in Jordan by Jordan National Press

ISBN: 978-1-84391-613-0

Contents

Foreword

The craft of the magician is to deceive; his art is to lead an audience into a place of wonder by transforming deception into drama. Houdini was the master of dramatic deception: at a time when economic shackles firmly restrained the imagination of his spectators, his symbolic escapes and defiant gestures must have touched upon something deeper than a mere pleasure in being fooled. The greatest magical conceits always seem to have resonated with their times: Selbit's Sawing In Half of the early 1920s is difficult to separate from the emerging Suffragette movement, the Parisian *Grand Guignol* theatre of horror which was flourishing in London following the grim shock of the First World War, and the new role of the heroine-in-jeopardy being explored by film and theatre (fashions were changing, too, and it would be easier to bundle the slimmer dress of an Edwardian lady into an illusion box than one of those billowing, hooped parachutes favoured by any Victorian dame hoping to be divided). Dull magic is a collection of tricks: great magic should sting.

The name 'Houdini' is synonymous with grand deception, and even the name is not all it seems. Houdini's real name was Erik Weisz: he took his assumed name from Jean-Eugène Robert-Houdin, a virtuoso clockmaker and the father of modern magic, a man with whom Harry had a tempestuous relationship. 'Houdini' means 'Of Houdin'. Harry's temperament sat at odds with the French conjuror's flair for literary exaggeration (Robert-Houdin's autobiography *The King of the Conjurors* is a sensational, semi-fictional romp and one of the greatest autobiographies ever written) and, ego oddly pricked, Houdini devoted much of his time to angrily exposing the ruses employed by his former hero.

Why should a magician wish to expose another's deceptions? It is an odd tendency, still rife amongst magicians today. The false displays of power and ludicrous posturing associated with the magician – generally at heart a lonely type who resorted to tricks at a young age to compensate for a lack of social confidence – do not sit well with encouraging a spectator's astonishment at a fellow (and potentially 'rival') magician. Rather than nurture the layman's delight in a successful illusion, and therefore celebrate the wonder and impossibility of it all (which ultimately helps all magicians), the preference amongst most conjurors is to immediately let it be known that they themselves can produce the same feat; that it is far easier than it appears; that the magician in question is really not quite as talented as he might have appeared. In a profession where appearance and misjudgement are the principal currencies, this is rather a bizarre and shameful tendency, though perhaps understandable given the kind of flatulent ego needed to pose as a miracle worker in the first place. For those in doubt, read the pages that follow: this book is full of bitter self-aggrandising and petty point-scoring from probably the greatest magician who ever lived.

There is, at least, an unspoken contract between magician and audience, according to which deception is both allowed and expected. In other areas, artful deception is practised without such a contract, such as that of the fraudulent psychic or medium, whom Houdini attacks vociferously in other works. The loss of his own mother, to whom Harry felt enormously close (he says, perhaps a little self-consciously, in these pages that he never travelled to Australia because he could not bear to be so far from her), and the fraud and failure he discovered while attempting to reach her through mediumistic channels, again lent the sharp sting of bitterness to his crusade to publicly expose those mediums deceiving the public. The mediums of the time were far more noteworthy than the limply unpleasant cold-readers known to us through television and radio today. The rational, scientific agenda of the Enlightenment had left a gap for the arcane and spiritual to flourish, while still demanding 'evidence' from those offering new paths to knowledge. Hence, the popular mediums of the latter half of the nineteenth century both found their lacuna in society and were obliged to produce physical 'proof' of the spirit contact they promised. For many years, tables levitated in the lightless séance room, spirit hands and ectoplasm drifted through the darkness, until the use of infra-red photography exposed the tricks of the mediums and their 'evidence' gradually shifted to the purely verbal illusions and dodges of the modern practitioners. This lack of physical 'proofs' of the modern medium has made the frauds more difficult to expose, and has most likely brought about far more well-intentioned psychics who do not consciously deceive at all, but instead honestly come to believe in their own professed powers. The capacity for self-deception, rarely acknowledged or understood by those who offer us supernatural answers to our problems, is huge: as easy as it is to make a medium's cold-reading statements 'fit' our own situation and come to believe that he must have some para-normal insight, it is hardly any more difficult for a would-be psychic with an average ego, upon hearing frequently positive feedback, to believe over time that he must be blessed with a special gift. It's harder to think you're doing it for real when you're tossing tambourines in the dark or have ready-made ectoplasm stuffed into your mouth or bottom.

The psychic has no contract with the audience that permits conscious fraud; the stage or close-up conjuror generally has a clear contract that permits all deception to take place to produce the final effect; the mind-reader or escapologist exists between the two and decides for himself how honest he wishes to be with his audience. The mind-reader frequently offers a nervous disclaimer – 'Everything you see is for entertainment only and I make no psychic claims' – generally this is no more than a reluctant legal get-out clause, as generally seen flashed up on the screen at the end of the shows of television psychics, but its message may be lost in the quite contradictory implications of the act itself. Escapologists such as Houdini also employ decep-tion, usually cartloads of it, but as the misleading of the public is less worrisome than with a medium, the issue is perhaps an artistic choice rather than a moral concern. But even with magicians, in whose case we expect to see (or, strictly speaking, not see) deception at work, we might feel that some contract of trust had been broken were we to find out that what was being presented as a card-sharp demonstration of virtuosic centre-deals and card-control was in fact an easy trick accomplished by far more mundane methods such as duplicate cards and so on. In a profession inextricable from deceit and whose end purpose is entertainment, there are no easy resolutions to these questions, and performers argue endlessly amongst themselves over what level of deception is permissible.

To all magicians (save perhaps those engrossed in the early career stages of mastering sleight-of-hand), the best deceptions are the biggest and boldest. Houdini betrays this delight in such stratagems when he talks with barely disguised admiration of the grand confidence tricks pulled off by some of the great characters described in these pages. The balls, the chutzpah, the gall, nerve and impudence of the successful lie that is huge enough to never be questioned is always a source of immense professional pleasure amongst magicians with any sense of the theatrical. And given that there is often a dose of envy bubbling within the moral outrage held by any one group for another, Houdini's famous pursuit of fraudsters is probably inseparable from a guilty resentment of their ability to masquerade and dissemble without limit.

To most of the audience, there is a delight in being fooled, and a granted unspoken licence for the magician to play the part of the mysterious wonder-worker we know he cannot be. This licence runs out when the magician becomes too enamoured with the role we have, as audience, allowed him to play. Unable to express his joy at the truly fascinating employments of misdirection and gimmickry that have secured his feats, the would-be Svengali must posture vacuously in order to secure the interest of his public. Stunts may become more self-aggrandising, public claims more ludicrous and the pretensions of a manufactured personality may start to grate. Part of the success of the modern duo Penn & Teller is that they have avoided playing the whimsical god role, which, as Teller has eloquently pointed out, is far less interesting than the contrasting figure of the very human, struggling hero. Deception alone has a limited shelf-life in terms of maintaining public enjoyment: replacing ego with an understanding of character, drama and what an audience wants is necessary for lasting popularity. Penn & Teller, now fifty-four and sixty respectively, are every bit as cool and fresh as they were when they became well known in the 1980s. Their recent, vociferous, highly successful *Bullshit!* series, exposing modern frauds from mediums to penis-enlargement schemes, would have made Houdini proud.

There will always be liars, swindlers and charlatans. Hopefully there will also always be the modern Houdinis and the seekers of truth, snapping at their heels and holding them to account. The knowledge of the magician, the escapologist, the gambling expert and the mentalist might keep us armed against thieves, lock-pickers, poker cheats and psychic fraudsters for some time to come. And as much as sceptics and fraudsters will fight bitterly to the end, they will remain bonded by ego, and the delight of deftly engineered deceit.

– Derren Brown, 2009

On Deception

Houdini on Houdini

How does he do it? That is the usual question I hear asked about my work in the theater. No, dear reader, it is not my purpose to tell you *how* I open locks, *how* I escape from a prison cell into which I have been locked, having previously been stripped naked and manacled with heavy irons. I do not intend to tell you in this book *how* I escape from the trunk or the tightly corded and nailed-up box in which I have been confined, or *how* I unlock any regulation handcuff that can be produced – not yet!

Some day I may tell all this, and then you will know. At present, I prefer that all who see me should draw their own conclusions. But exactly how I accomplish these things I shall still leave you to guess, gentle reader. I should not want you to go into the show business. It's a hard life, so they say.

'Have you ever been stuck at it?' I think I hear you ask. Not yet. I have had some pretty close calls, but have always pulled through somehow. The nearest I ever came to giving in was during my engagement at Blackbourne, England. There I offered a prize to the man who could fasten me in such a way that I could not escape. One man accepted my challenge. He was an instructor in athletics, and was out for blood. He evidently looked upon my challenge as a personal affront to him. At any rate, he started in to shackle me.

He first handcuffed my hands in front, then locked elbow irons, the chain of which went behind my back. Then he handcuffed my legs, and after this bent me backward and chained my back and feet together. I had to kneel down. Every chain and handcuff was fitted to the limit. I started in, but at the end of an hour I suffered so under the strain that I asked to be let out. My back was aching, my circulation was stopped in my wrists, and my arms became paralyzed. My opponent's only reply was, 'This is a bet. Cry quits or keep on.'

The music hall where I was playing was packed, and while watching me became fairly wild. I kept on, but I was only about half conscious. Every joint in my body was aching, and I had but little use of my arms. I asked as a favor that he free my hands long enough for the circulation to start again, but he only laughed and exclaimed, 'This is no love affair, this is a contest. Say you are defeated and I'll release you.'

I gritted my teeth and went at it once more. For two hours and a half I exerted myself, fighting for my professional good name. In the meanwhile, the audience was cheering itself hoarse. Some cried 'Give it up,' and others, 'Keep on, you'll do it.' I don't believe any such scene was ever acted in a theater. The house was crazy with excitement, and I was covered with blood brought on by my exertion to release myself and chaffing irons. But I did it. I got free of every chain and handcuff. Then they had to carry me off the stage, and I suffered from the effects for months afterwards.

As for the prison cell, I have never been locked in one I could not open. I have had the honor of making my escape from securely locked cells in jails, prisons and police stations in almost every large city in the world, and under the most rigid conditions. The chiefs of police, the wardens, the jailers, the detectives, and citizens who have been present at these tests know that they are real and actual. Perhaps the most historic American feat that gained for me the most notoriety was my escape in January 1906, from Cell 2, Murderers' Row, in the United States Jail at Washington, D.C.; from the very cell in which Guiteau, the assassin of President Garfield, was confined until he was led forth to be hanged. Since my return from abroad in October 1905, I have escaped, after being locked up in a nude state, from cells in New York City, Brooklyn, Detroit, Rochester, Buffalo, Washington, Baltimore, Philadelphia, Providence, and city tombs in Boston and Lowell. In all cases I submitted to a close search, being stark naked and heavily manacled into the cell, which was also thoroughly searched.

I am an American by birth, born in Appleton, Wisconsin, U.S.A., on 6th April 1873. To my lot have fallen more experiences, more strange adventures, more ups and downs, in my thirty-three years of life than to most men.

When about nine years of age my mother, to whom I am greatly attached, apprenticed me to a mechanic to learn that trade; but, after an uneventful term with the tools of the trade, I resolved to see the world with my own eager eyes. So I ran away from home, and in this way made an early acquaintance with the corrugated side of life.

I joined a small circus, and soon learned to conduct the Punch and Judy show, to do a ventriloquial act, and to play town clown on the bars – 'gol darn it.' I also doubled in brass – that is, I beat the cymbals. I here gained the experiences that possibly ripened me into the world's Handcuff King and Prison Breaker – a title which I have justly earned.

But there was a time when I was not recognized as I am now. Those were the days of small things. That was in the Middle West. After that, London and an engagement at the Alhambra. After that, everywhere on the continent and all over America. I have not yet been to Australia. I do not wish to be so far away from my mother.

While touring Germany I brought suit against the police and a newspaper because they said my act was not genuine. I won the case – to have lost it would have meant ruin. Again, in Russia, I was bound by the officials of the spy police and locked in a Siberian transport cell. Had I failed to escape, I would have been compelled to journey to Siberia, as the key that locks these cells does not open them. The governor-general in Siberia has the only key to open them. I was out in twenty minutes.

If there were more room in this book I would like to tell you of the many places in which I have played, both in America and Europe. I have many certificates from police officials. I was almost too busy to write this book, although I have been collecting the material for a long time. But now I am pleased it is written, and trust it may please you. I believe that the reading of this book will so familiarize the public with the methods of the criminal classes that it will enable law-abiding citizens to protect themselves from the snares of the evil-doer.

I hope it will warn you away from crime and all evil-doing. It may tell the 'Right Way to Do Wrong', but, as I said in the beginning, all I have to say is 'Don't'.

Sincerely yours,

Harry Houdini

Thieves and Their Tricks

A thief is one who appropriates any kind of property or money to his own use without the consent of the owner. As distinguished from a burglar, a thief does not break into a house or enter in the nighttime, but takes his plunder wherever he can find it. A thief may gain entrance to a house and steal a valuable diamond, but he uses his sharp wits to pass the door instead of the burglar's jimmy and skeleton keys.

There are thieves of various kinds, from the common sneak thief and shoplifter to the expert pickpocket and clever swindler, who sometimes makes hauls amounting to many thousands of dollars. The use of the word 'thief' however is generally confined to such classes of criminals as shoplifters, pickpockets and the like. Overcoat thieves ply their trade in the residential sections of the city. They will sometimes ring the front doorbell and ask for the master or mistress of the house, giving some plausible pretext, and usually the name of the party living there. While the servant has gone to tell the mistress of the caller, he quietly picks up what garments are in sight on the hat rack and makes off with them.

The Venetian blind thief got his name from the practice of the English thieves of making the pretext that they had come to repair the blinds of the house. A thief will call at the door claiming to be a mechanic to look over the house for necessary repairs, and in his rounds will gather up any valuable article that he can lay his hands on. This class of rascal even impersonates the plumber or the gas inspector with equally successful results.

Thieves at church are a very common occurrence. A case is related in London not long ago where a chapel had been furnished with one hundred new Bibles. They were first used at the afternoon service, and when the congregation gathered for evening they had all disappeared. A very common experience of church officers is to find that books disappear gradually; not only books, but hassocks and cushions are taken from houses of worship. Petty robberies from the collection box are not infrequent. In some localities the custom of covering one's offering with one's hand so that other worshipers shall not see the amount given gives the thief his opportunity, for in the rapid passing of the plate it is easy for the skilful professional thief to put in a penny and at the same moment take out a dollar. This is sometimes done by a sticky substance put upon a single finger. Umbrella thieves and pickpockets also ply their trade in church as well as in other places of public gathering.

'How can you detect a church thief?' is a question I have often asked detectives. There seems to be no real answer; but, as a general rule, it is just as well to look out for your property as carefully when you are in church as when you are out.

Thieves as wedding guests

There is scarcely a fashionable wedding where the contracting parties are wealthy that does not suffer from the presence of wedding thieves. For this reason, the more expensive items of jewelry are often imitated in paste before they are put on exhibition among the gifts, while the originals are sent to the bank. The wedding-gift lifter works his game as follows: disguised as a tradesman or assistant, he gains the confidence of the servants, gets a description of a diamond tiara, or other article of great value, which he then has a duplicate set of made with imitation paste diamonds. He will even go as far as to pay fifteen or a hundred dollars for a good imitation article. Armed with this and perfectly dressed, he makes his way among the party of guests and finds it no great risk to adroitly change the counterfeit for the genuine jewel.

Trick of the Van Thief

Vans that are covered entirely with tarpaulin or canvas, and have a loose back, present opportunities to the van thief. A favorite trick is for the thief to wheel a hand cart, covered with sacking, under which a confederate lies concealed, behind one of these vans. The confederate quickly puts the upper part of his body inside the van, his feet remaining in the cart. Being concealed from view by the loose tarpaulin, he seizes a package, dropping back with it into the cart, which is pushed off at once. A wet day is preferred for this trick, as then not so many people are about, and the driver is likely to be holding his head down as a protection from the rain, in consequence of which he will not look behind.

The Trick Satchel Thieves

It is when the dark days come round that the railway-station thief most safely conducts his operations. The summer tourist he loves not, for his luggage contains few valuables, and there is then too much light about. A dull afternoon and well-to-do people going off by train are what the platform prowler asks for. And here is shown as a warning, if needs be, an artful appliance that station thieves have used of late years. It looks like an ordinary portmanteau; and so it is with a difference.

It is a specially-made portmanteau, the bottom of which closes up on pressure being applied. Thus, when the 'trick' portmanteau is placed over a smaller one that lies upon the platform, the larger one comes down as a cover over it. By a movement of the thumb of the hand that holds the portmanteau handle, powerful springs are released which tightly grasp the portmanteau that is inside, and it can thus be carried away completely enveloped from sight.

If, therefore, you see a suspicious-looking character hanging about, don't set him down as a genuine passenger just because he has a bag.

Diamond in a Chew of Gum

One of the cleverest and most unscrupulous diamond thieves I ever heard of perfected a scheme for daylight robbery of un-mounted gems which, for a time simply, defied detectives of London and Paris. The game was played as follows: a lady, well-dressed and looking like a respectable and wealthy matron who might be the wife of a banker or large merchant, enters a jewelry store and asks to see some un-mounted diamonds. The clerk shows her the stones, and while she is looking at them, a second lady equally respectable in appearance enters and approaches the same Counter. She seems to be interested in diamonds.

Suddenly one of the most valuable gems is missing. The proprietor is summoned, the detectives rush in, and an officer is called. The women, who both declare their innocence, are carefully searched, but the diamond has absolutely disappeared. Eventually both the women are released, but the diamond is never recovered.

The way the trick was played is this: one of the women (both of whom are members of the gang) deftly concealed the diamond in a piece of chewing gum and sticks it on the under side of the front edge of the counter. There it remains safely hidden away while the frantic search is going on. A third member of the gang slips in afterward with the crowd of curious and removes the gum containing the diamond and makes off with it.

Begging Letters and Swindles

Every section of the country, almost every city, has one or more begging-letter writers, who ply their trade with greater or less success, and exercise their arts upon the simple and credulous.

These clever rascals range all the way from the ignorant crook that writes a pitiful story of want and misery, and who neither receives nor expects more than a few dollars at a time, to the master of the craft, who goes about it like a regular business, has a well-organized office and a force of stenographers and clerks, who are kept busy day in and day out sending off and receiving mail.

Several remarkable cases have been unearthed only lately, where the fake was receiving hundreds of letters daily, the large majority of them containing money. The post office authorities, however, have been getting after this class of rogues very sharply of late, and any organized plundering by the use of the mails, is almost certain to come to an untimely end sooner or later.

If anyone has reason to believe that a business of the kind is conducted on fraudulent lines, a complaint to one of the post office inspectors in any large city will quickly bring a 'fraud order' against the party, restraining them from use of the mails, and a rigid investigation follows. Then the game is up, and it's back to the 'tall timber' for them. It is a well-known fact, however, that this recourse to the 'fraud order' is frequently used by unprincipled persons, out of spite and to obtain revenge upon those who are actually conducting a legitimate business. The fraudulent advertisement is often an adjunct to the bogus letter scheme, and designed to get names of those to whom a special kind of letter may be written. One of the most daring schemes of this kind was unearthed a short time ago in New York City. A man fitted up a suite of offices in elegant style in one of the large office buildings. He then traveled to South Dakota, and under the laws of that State, incorporated a stock company, with a capitalization of five million dollars. It was called a commercial and mining company. Returning to New York, he instructed the Press Clipping Bureau to save him the obituary notices of all males that died in the States other than New York – just far enough away from the center of operations to be comfortable for him.

Using these obituary notices for guides, he would write to the dead man, notifying him that the last payment was due on the five hundred or one thousand shares of stock which he had bought at fifty cents a share. He congratulated the man on his foresight on investing in this stock, as it had gone up several points, and was still rising in value. He begged that a remittance in final payment of this stock should be sent at once.

A beautifully engrossed certificate of stock was enclosed in the letter to the dead man, and the inevitable result was that the surviving relatives, thinking the departed one had bought this stock quietly and forgotten to mention it, sent on a check for all the way from one hundred to five hundred dollars as requested. It was one of the prettiest schemes that has been worked for a long time, and the actual amount of money realized by the swindler will never be known. Such a 'snap' could not last long, however, and the promulgator of the swindle was soon detected and brought to trial.

One man advertised to sell ten yards of good silk for twenty-five cents, and so worded his announcement as to suggest a bankrupt sale or smuggled goods. For a time he reaped a rich harvest. Money came thick and fast. To each of his dupes he mailed ten yards of sewing silk!

Another rascal offered a complete and perfect sewing machine for one dollar. He, also, gathered in the dollars at a rapid rate, till Uncle Sam put a stop to his operations – he sent his victims a common sewing needle!

This is quite in line with the fellow who advertised a few years ago to tell a sure way of getting rid of chinch bugs for one dollar. After the victim had sent the dollar, he received by mail a card upon which was printed the following,

Catch the chinch bug. Hold it by the legs carefully between the thumb and forefinger. Lay its head on the anvil, and hit it with a hammer as hard as you can.

Many of these advertisements are inserted merely to receive names and addresses of credulous people. The lists of names are then sold or rented out to fake mail-order houses, who proceed to circularize them.

Chain-letter schemes are now declared illegal, but for some time a number of clever dodges of this kind were worked throughout the United States as well as on the continent. A brief description of one of these schemes will show the character of this kind of enterprise. The scheme was where a trip to the Paris Exposition, with two hundred dollars for expenses, was offered as a prize. Each person entering the contest was required to pay thirty cents, then send to friends two letters, requesting them to send their names to the original promoter, and send duplicate letters to two of their friends, the operation to be repeated indefinitely.

Each person writing to the original promoter was to receive an offer, allowing him to start a chain on his own account, on payment of thirty cents, the trip and money going to the one whose chain brings out the largest number of letters. The ostensible object was to secure names for employment at the Exposition.

Fake, Fake, Fake

There are certain classes of men, and women too, who, while not actually criminal, are yet so close to the boundary line in their practices as to need some special mention in this book. Take, for instance, the many so-called 'divine' or mental healers, who pretend to cure all sorts of diseases by the laying on of hands or simply absent treatment, or the old-style patent medicine fraud who retailed sweetened and colored water under some high-sounding name, as Dr So and So's Elixir and Tonic, from the tail end of a cart, after having attracted a crowd of the curious with a lecture or open-air minstrel show.

Far be it from me to decry the actual healing and curative value of many excellent proprietary medicines and preparations on the market today. But, among the good, there are many that are worthless, and I should advise my readers to take such 'remedies' only on the advice of their family physician.

The fake 'doctor' is still with us, and his advertisements are often to be seen in the newspapers of America. They usually advertise under some honest-sounding name, and assume all the titles and learned degrees of two continents. Some are actually physicians, and, failing in the regular practice, have set out to make a living by deluding suffering humanity. It would be amusing, if it were not sorrowful, to see the crowds of patients who bring their ailments to such 'doctors'. The game is to give the sufferer some relief at first, in order to encourage him, and then prolong his case through many weary weeks and months, until they have gotten all the money he can afford to spend. Such doctors usually call themselves 'specialists', but their real specialty is in exhorting money from their dupes, and my advice is to keep as far away from them as possible.

Thanks to the energetic efforts of the authorities many, if not all, of these practitioners have been driven out, and it is to be hoped that such tragedies as that unearthed in the Susan Geary case will be rare in the future.[1]

The case of Francis Truth, alias Will Bemis, the self-styled Divine Healer, attracted no little attention throughout the East, especially in Boston, a few years ago. The man was a handsome, plausible, smooth-spoken man, who claimed to have some mysterious mesmeric power by which he could cure any disease, simply by the laying on of hands. His advertisements bristled with testimonials and brilliant promises, and he did a good business among the credulous. Many, who doubtless had nothing whatever the matter with them, were hypnotized into the belief that they were cured.

Finally, Truth – or Bemis – found his money getting limited, because he could only 'treat' a limited number a day. Then he had recourse to the absent-treatment dodge. He would tell his patients that he would give them an absent treatment at a certain hour, and at that time they were to retire to their rooms and think of him, and they would receive the healing influence! As the number of his dupes grew, he branched into a mail-order feature, until hundreds and thousands of people who had never seen the 'healer' were sending him money by mail. He received hundreds of letters each day, until the post office was forced to deliver them in great bags, and his income amounted to thousands of dollars a week! Truth lived in great style, drove about in his own carriage, had quite an office force of stenographers and clerks to handle the mail, and was getting rich, hand over fist, when the post office authorities and the police put an end to his career.

Advertising mediums, clairvoyants, and astrologers have hosts of dupes, and some invite the methods of the confidence man, with mystical advice and fortune telling. Not long ago, a certain Miss Ethel L–, of Malden, Massachusetts, visited a so-called medium in Boston. As soon as she entered his inner sanctum she was surprised to have him caution her about a large sum of money which she was carrying. This 'occult' knowledge so inspired her confidence, that she asked his advice about a suit she was interested in. He told her he would have to put her in a trance, which he did. When she came out of it, he cautioned her to go directly home, and to *hold her fingers crossed* until she reached her own room, where she must remain for two days. It was actually some hours before she realized that she had been robbed of a thousand dollars which she had in her pocket! Of course, the medium had disappeared!

I must say that with all its boasted culture and learning, Boston seems to be a favorite city for all sorts of schemes of this kind; astrologers, mediums, clairvoyants, test-mediums, and the like abound in the Hub as in few other places it has been my good fortune to visit, and I have been all over the world. Chicago also has its share.

New Yorkers pride themselves in believing in nothing at all, and yet it was only a short time ago that a man named Ridgley, and calling himself the East Indian Mystery, victimized many people of wealth and fashion in that metropolis. This remarkable person combined the fakir of the East with the modern magnetic healer and the Voodoo doctor of French Louisiana. The man himself is seventy years old. He is small, spry, alert, and wonderfully shrewd. His beard is bushy and black, except where age has whitened the edges, and grows thick and curly at the sides. The nose is as flat as a Negro's. He denies Negro blood, however, and abhors the race. He claims to be from Hindustan, and talks to others in the house in a strange tongue.

The eyes of the man are small, shrewd, and dark. The forehead, from each side of which grows gray, bushy hair that hides the ears, is high, receding, and intelligent. 'I knew you were coming,' says this wizard-like man, 'and I determined to receive you though warned against you. Now you want to know what I am, what I do. Let us be honest with each other.'

He chooses big words as he proceeds to describe himself. They are used aptly, but mispronounced. The 'th' becomes 'd', and there are other things not unfamiliar in the Southern negro. The East Indian proceeds to read your character and to tell you of your life. He does it well.

'I am not a fortune teller,' he explains. 'They are frauds, and I am a physiognomist. I read from the apex of the nose to the top of the forehead. I don't predict; I tell you; and I don't ask you to say if I am right or wrong.'

It is said that among this man's patrons have been men and women whose names are a part of the life of New York. It is also said that a recent marriage which astonished New York society came after the woman in the case had consulted this strange combination of charlatan and physician. She confided to him her desire, told him of her repeated failures to secure her wish, took the treatment, and in three months was married. Then followed, so the story goes, many presents, among them a tenement, to the East Indian.

Spiritualism has many followers, and at one time I was almost a believer, but this was before I made a thorough investigation, which I have followed up even to the present day. I have never seen a materialization or a manifestation which I cannot fully explain. Of course, I cannot explain those that I 'hear' about, as no two people see the same one thing alike.

Spiritualism is really a beautiful belief for those that are honest and believe in it; but as I have visited the greatest spiritualistic meetings in the world, I am sorry to say that no one has ever produced anything for me that would smack of the spiritual.

In Germany, spirit mediums are put in jail for obtaining money under false pretences. In England, Maskenlyne, of Maskenlyne & Cook, has done a great deal to keep the so-called fraud spiritualistic mediums out of England. In the future, I contemplate writing a book on spiritualistic methods, and how they do their tricks. I do not mean genuine spiritualists who have no tricks, but those mediums who use their knowledge of magic to gain a living.

The Davenport Brothers, during their short but strenuous career, had a terrible time of it in their journeys abroad. They were driven out of England, but they made enough money to last them the rest of their lives.

Light on the Subject of Jailbreaking

I am induced to take this step for the manifest reason that the public of both hemispheres may, through ignorance of the real truth, give credence to the mendacious boasts and braggadocio of the horde of imitators who have sprung into existence with mushroom rapidity of growth, and equal flimsiness of vital fiber, and who, with amazing effrontery and pernicious falsity, seek to claim and hold the credit and honor, such as they may be, that belong to me.

It is in the same spirit and for the same cogent reason, I execute my present duty of duly setting forth my right to the title which I hold and the absolute pilfering of name, fame, and the other emoluments of success by those others who advertise and rate as 'Handcuff Kings', 'Jail Breakers', etc, *ad libitum*, *ad nauseam*.

That I have a horde of imitators may not be as well known as it will be to those who have the patience and the sense of fairness sufficiently developed to lead them to read this article through to its conclusion.

Therefore it will not be considered unbecoming of me to set here the details of my conception, execution, and performance of the Challenge Handcuff and Escape Act as presented by time in the principal vaudeville and music hall theaters of Europe and America. And I trust also that I will not be deemed guilty of undue egotism, or of having an attack of 'exaggerated of ego', to borrow a popular term growing out of the Thaw trial, if I assert that this act has proved to be the greatest drawing card and longest lived sensation that has ever been offered in annals of the stage. This has been demonstrated by the record-breaking attendance in every theater in which I have given the act, either in part or whole, and also by the duration of my engagement in the principal theaters among those in which I have been booked.

'Art is long and life is short,' says the ancient poet. The stage and its people, in the light of history, make this a verity. As examples, take the famous Davenport Brothers, also the 'Georgia Magnet', also the 'Bullet-Proof Man', etc. For the benefit of those who have not heard of the latter sensational attraction – which was indeed a great novelty for a limited time – I will explain that the man was a German who claimed to possess a coat that was impervious to bullets. He would don this coat and allow anyone to shoot a bullet of any caliber at him. One day a marksman shot him below the coat, in the groin, and he eventually died from the wounds inflicted. His last request was that his beloved invention be buried with him. This, however, was not granted, for it was thought due to the world that an invention should be made known. The coat, on being ripped open, was found stuffed or padded with powdered glass.

Returning to the subject of my own career, I assert here with all the positiveness I can command that I am the originator of the Challenge Handcuff Act, which consists in the artist's inviting any person in his audience to submit handcuffs of his own from which the performer must release himself. And it is proper that I should add at this point that I do not claim to have conceived and originated the simple handcuff trick. Every novice in this line knows that it has been done for many years, or so far back, as lawyers say, 'that memory runneth not to the contrary'.

French historians of the stage show that as far back as 1700, La Tude performed it. Pinetti did chain releases in 1780, and other modern magicians have had it in their programs since 1825. The Senor Bologna, instructor of John Henry Anderson, made a small trick out of it. Anderson placed it among his repertoire the second time he came to America in 1861 and when exposing the Davenport Brothers, he made quite a feature of it. In fact, I have an old monthly of 1870 in which a handcuff trick is explained in an article exposing spirit mediums.

Dr Redmond who, I hear, is still very much alive in England, made quite a reputation as a rope expert and handcuff manipulator in 1872–3, and I have several interesting bills of his performances.

Few give me credit, but had I been able to copyright my new tricks, they would all have to pay me a royalty.

But as such cannot be done, the only thing I ask of the numerous imitators is to give credit where credit is due.

No one, to my knowledge, performs my tests according to my method except my brother Theo Hardeen, as they ALL resort to fakery and collusion in presenting to the public that which they wish to have thought is exactly as Houdini performs his challenges.

The following challenges have been performed by myself, some are very interesting. Release in full view of the audience from straitjackets used on murderous insane; the nailed up in the packing case escape; the packing case built on the stage; the paper bag; the willow hamper; the hamper swung in the air; the steel unprepared cage or basket; riveted into a steel water boiler; hung to a ladder in mid-air; nailed to a door; escape from unprepared glass box; out of a large football; release from a large mail pouch; escape from a roll top desk; escape from a zinc-lined piano box, etc. In fact during long engagements, I have accepted a different challenge for every performance.

In order to stop all controversy concerning this jailbreaking affair, I shall publish the methods that have been used by some of those who will stop at nothing in order to willfully deceive the public.

First of all, there is a young man who calls himself Brindemour who, according to all I can learn, claims to be the originator of jailbreaking and has accused me of stealing the material from him. He has even gone so far as to say that I assisted him. Why, in 1896 I visited Woonsocket, R.I., with a show and made quite the handcuff act. There I met a photographer whose name was George W. Brown. He made himself known to me and informed me that he was an amateur magician, and that at certain periods of the year he gave performances for friends and lodges. His great hit was to impersonate a ballet girl.

He showed me pictures of himself in ballet costume and seemed to be proud that he could impersonate the female sex so perfectly. That was in 1896. About a year later, after purchasing a bunch of handcuff keys, this Brown called himself Brindemour. He gave a trial show at Keith's Providence house for Manager Lovenberg and failed to make good. His great stunt then was to make church bells ring, which is accomplished with a confederate and was Sig. Blitz's standby.[2] At any rate, the Great Brindemour failing to make good, followed me into Philadelphia and started to expose his handcuff act. He did this in Providence, also Philadelphia, and made a dismal failure. The effect of his work showed him that he was on the wrong track, and eventually he did expose the few fake tricks that he had and went into it without the exposures.

He pursued the same old groove until I returned to America, when he deliberately copied all of my challenges as best he could. I wondered how he did his jailbreaking stunts, as I knew he could no more pick a lock than the Czar of Russia will give the Russian newspapers the right of free press. Recently I ascertained the facts as to several of his escapes, or rather their 'mysterious means', and I will give the reader the benefit of my investigations. At the same time I invite the closest investigation of anything that I have ever done. While filling an engagement at Albaugh's Theatre, Baltimore, Brindemour escaped from the cells at police headquarters under the following circumstances. A reporter on the *Baltimore News*, by name of 'Clint' MacCabe, called on Harry Schanberger, who is engaged in an official position at police headquarters (this incident was told me personally by Harry Schanberger and in the presence of witnesses). MacCabe, after a chat with Harry Schanberger, borrowed the set of keys from Schanberger, telling him that he wanted to give them to Brindemour, so that he could give a press performance and make the people believe that Brindemour had escaped 'on the square'.

Schanberger loaned MacCabe the two keys, and naturally Brindemour escaped from the police headquarters cells, using the genuine keys that belong to the Police Department. And he dares to call himself the police mystifier!

In my mind I can almost hear the spirit of poor Chas. Bertram say, 'Isn't that wonderful?'[3] The strange thing about this affair is that in Baltimore, another alleged jail breaker met his quietus for the time being.

He is Cunning, who also labors under the delusion that he is the original world's greatest. I quote from the *Baltimore News*, and it will be seen how much 'talent' this gentleman possesses.

Extract from the Baltimore News, Thursday, February 8, 1906:

Cunning's Game Exposed

Cunning, the hitherto mysterious opener of handcuffs and shackles, who is exhibiting at the Monumental Theatre this week, was found out today by Acting Turnkey John Lanahan at the Central Station and had to abandon the feat that he had promised to do of escaping from a locked cell.

Before being locked in the cell, Cunning went into the latter, pretending to examine it and secretly placed a key upon a ledge, but Lanahan discovered the key just as Cunning was about to be locked in, and when told of the discovery, the wizard said, 'You've got me,' admitted that he could not open the cell without a key, and abandoned the exhibition.

The real truth of this jailbreak is that Mr Joe Kernan went to the police captain and borrowed the keys and handed them to Cunning. The turnkey, Lanahan, not being in the 'know', discovered the palpable 'planting' of the keys and ran with them to the captain. In this way the 'stunt' was unexpectedly exposed.

Personally, I think it ought to be a prison offense for any official to loan his keys to these would-be and so-called mystifiers, and if managers wish to lend themselves willfully to deceive their audience, the quicker they find out that they are treading the wrong path the better for them, too. You can take any stagehand, and in five minutes make just as good a jail-breaker as the many that are now trading on my name.

Another 'gross' mis-representer is a youth named Grosse. This man, or rather youth, claims that he can open time lock safes and all the complicated locks of the world, stating that handcuffs are mere play to him. Why, he can't even pick his teeth, and if he were put to a test with a lock picker, I doubt that he could even throw back a one tumbler lock. Yes, he would have trouble to pull back a common latch.

No doubt some of the police that are entangled with some these jailbreakers will grow hot under the collar at me for show-ing this thing up, but as long as these fellows are pretending to do my work, and as long as they stoop to do it in this manner, just so long will I publish the real facts as soon as I find them out.

In conclusion, I wish to state that I defy any manager or police official to come forward and prove that I, by any under-hand means or conniving methods, have stooped or lowered my manhood to ask them willfully to deceive the public by such misrepresentations.

The Straitjacket Release

The word straitjacket alone conjures up to the mind pictures of violent maniacs and thoughts that tend to gruesome channels.

The origin of the presentation of this release on the stage occurred to me during the season of 1894–5, while touring the Canadian provinces where I went to fulfill an engagement with Marco, the magician (now James Dooley of Hartford, Conn.). The company fared disastrously, because a man had assumed the name of Marco and the preceding season toured through the territory giving so poor a show that the audiences went away complaining. When the real Marco company arrived, they sparingly patronized us, but as they left, we could hear remarks all over to the effect that 'this is not the same Marco we had here last time.' The name of the bogus Marco was, I believe, Skinner, and the people said it was actually one well-earned and appropriate for the kind of show he presented to them.

Our show closed in Halifax, Nova Scotia, and I thereupon determined to proceed by myself and give the whole show. While in St Johns, I met a Dr Steeves, who then was in charge of a large insane asylum, and received an invitation from him to visit his institution, which I accepted. After showing me the various wards, he eventually showed me the padded cells, in one of which through the small bars of the cell door, I saw a maniac struggling on the canvas padded floor, rolling about and straining each and every muscle in a vain attempt to get his hands over his head and striving in every conceivable manner to free himself from his canvas restraint which I later on learned was called a straitjacket.

Entranced, I watched the efforts of this man, whose struggle caused beads of perspiration to roll off him, and from where I stood, I noted that were he able to dislocate his arms at the shoulder joint, he would have been able to cause his restraint to become slack in certain parts allowing him to free his arms. But, as it was that the straps were drawn tight, the more he struggled, the tighter his restraint encircled him, and eventually he lay exhausted, panting, and powerless to move.

Previous to this incident I had seen and used various restraints such as insane restraint muffs, belts, bed-straps, etc, but this was the first time I saw a straitjacket, and it left so vivid an impression my mind that I hardly slept that night, and in such moments as I slept, I saw nothing but straitjackets, maniacs, and padded cells! In the wakeful part of the night, I wondered what the effect would be to an audience to have them see a man placed in a straitjacket and watch him force himself free therefrom.

The very next morning I obtained permission to try to escape from one, and during one entire week, I practiced steadily and then presented it on the stage and made my escape therefrom behind a curtain. I pursued this method for some time, but it was so often repeated to me that people seeing me emerge from the cabinet after my release with hair disheveled, countenance covered with perspiration, trousers covered with dust, and ofttimes even my clothes being torn, remarked, 'Oh, he is faking it, it did not take all that effort to make his escape,' that eventually I determined to show to the audience exactly what means I resorted to to effect my release and so did the straitjacket release in full view of everybody.

The straitjacket is made of strong brown canvas or sail cloth and has a deep leather collar and leather cuffs; these cuffs are sewn up at the ends, making a sort of bag into which each arm is placed; the seams are covered with leather bands attached to which are leather straps and steel buckles which, when strapped upon a person, fit and buckle up in back. The sleeves of this jacket are made so long that when the arms of the wearer are placed in them and folded across the chest, the leather cuffs of the sleeves, to which are attached straps and buckles, meet at the back of the body, one overlapping the other. The opening of the straitjacket is at the back where several straps and buckles are sewn which are fastened at the back.

The first step necessary to free yourself is to place the elbow, which has the continuous band *under* the opposite elbow, on some solid foundation, and by sheer strength, to exert sufficient force at this elbow so as to force it gradually toward the head, and by further persistent straining, you eventually force the head under the *lower arm*, which results in bringing both of the encased arms in front of the body. (It is very important that these instructions be followed closely step by step; and when placing the arms across the chest, sufficient care must be observed simply to place one arm on top of the other and not have them inter-locked.)

Once having freed your arms to such an extent as to get them in front of your body, you can now undo the buckles of the straps of your cuffs with your teeth, after which you open the buckles at the back with your hands which are still encased in the canvas sleeves, and then you remove the straitjacket from your body.

There are various kinds of straitjacket made from different materials, some being entirely made of leather; and, of course, the more inflexible the material, the more difficult is your release and the longer the time required.

In 1901, Count Schwerin, then chief of police of Hanover, had his warders place me in a straitjacket from which it took me one hour and twenty-nine minutes to effect my release. The pain, torture, agony, and misery of that struggle will forever live in my mind.

There is a peregrinating impostor in Germany who escapes from a straitjacket from which any child could make its escape. He has it made of pliable white canvas with very long sleeves and short body, though when strapped on him, it seems as if he were firmly secured. In making his escape, he goes through fantastic gyrations and eventually wriggles out of his fastenings.

The American imitators, as a rule, improvise a straitjacket that they can pull over their heads. Of course, these latter two are trick straitjackets and should not be confounded with the genuine ones.

Skeleton Keys

Such keys are made for opening a set or series of locks each of which has a different make of key so that one key will not open another lock in the set, yet, the holder of the master or skeleton key will open all. In old locks with fixed wards, this was done by making the wards of a slightly different form and yet such that the skeleton would pass them all.

It is always possible to find the shape of the wards by merely putting in a blank key covered with wax and pressing it against them. When this was done, it was by no means necessary to cut out the key in the complicated form of the ward, because no part of that key does any work except the edge farthest from the pipe, and so a key in the shape of the next one would do just as well; and a small collection of skeleton keys, as they are called, of a few different patterns were all the stock in trade that a lock picker required.

Some wardlock pickers are adjustable. The bits fit into holes in the shank of the key and are secured by screws, so that you can regulate them to whatever size you require for the lock you wish to open.

There are some simple yet very useful lock pickers, and while a number of them look very much like each other, they are of different sizes so as to lift the tumblers and throw back the bolt. I used four in my celebrated lawsuit at Cologne, with which I picked hundreds of three and four lever locks almost as quickly as they could be opened with a key, for I practiced every day and night for three months on these particular locks.

The lock used in Germany on the regulation transportation chain is of a peculiar three or four lever pattern. The post in the keyhole prohibits a strong pick from entering, so I made several different pickers from piano wire.

This was thin and very stiff, for I knew in order to win my lawsuit I would have to open any lock that was placed before me, and started in to practice. The best practice I could obtain was to procure a position as a repair locksmith in a small shop. In Berlin,

I knew a locksmith, Mueller, who has a shop on Mittle Strasse, and he was more than willing that I should work for nothing, and I commenced repairing locks for him. He soon discovered that his thirty-five years of experience as a locksmith was nothing as compared to my trick in opening locks, and he soon had a thriving trade for his young man to open locks. In order that I should know the exact heights of the various locks used on the police chains, he ordered a great gross, and soon exchanged them for another great gross of other patterns, etc. In that way I would pass six to ten hours daily picking locks and soon, with the assistance of the four picks, I could open any lock that contained the five or six Chubb levers. The 'gateways' were never made close, as is the case in fine lever locks, so it became a very simple matter for me to open each and every lock which was made on that principle, and very handy that experience was in court.

I found I could facilitate matters by taking an ordinary elastic garter and fastening it to the clasp of the padlock and looping the other end to my foot so that by stretching the elastic and holding the lock in the left hand, I would have a pull on the clasp. Now by inserting the lockpicker, I could lift one lever after the other until all were of the proper height, when the elastic, like a faithful servant, at the proper time pulled the clasp back, which freed from the bolt, and thereby caused the lock to open.

Just at this juncture, it is not out of place to describe the German transport chain which is used by the German police almost exclusively for transporting prisoners. The chain has two rings, one for each hand, one being located at the end of the chain and the other in the center. One lock is utilized for securing both hands, the chain entwines both wrists which rest one above the other.

After the chain has been fastened on your wrist, the first movement is to bring each arm lengthwise on the other, the fingers of both hands pointing towards the opposite elbows, and by sheer force of strength, you extricate yourself from the chain one hand at a time.

Lock Picking Implements

In no country have I found so many expensive locks in use as in France; almost every door is equipped with a six-lever Chubb or Bramah lock. Crooks would have an exceptionally hard time to pick such locks, so they resort to the quicker and easier method of forcing the doors with heavy chisels.

A daring criminal, a French murderer whose specialty was robbing churches, was caught by the merest accident. He laid plans for a cool and premeditated murder of the Geldbrief Träger in Berlin, which class of postmen carry only money sent by mail and sometimes are entrusted with large sums.

This man, Olschansky, sent through the mail to himself one hundred marks (about twenty-five dollars) having previously hired a small room in a street where the house was almost empty of lodgers.

The room was on the top floor, and when the postman arrived Monday morning, he found Olschansky awaiting him, and to all intents and purposes, Olschansky was just seated at his morning lunch (which all Germany partakes of about ten o'clock) consisting of bottled beer and sandwiches.

Olschansky offered the postman a bottle of beer, but gave him no glass. He was then compelled to drink out of the bottle, and as the bottle was raised to his lips, Olschansky raised a heavy board and drove the bottle down the postman's throat, and then immediately struck him over the temple and kept on hitting the stunned man until he had beaten the life out of his body.

He took all the money from the leather bag carried by the postman, locked the door, and left the building.

But he forgot to pay the beer man, and instead of going about his business, he went to pay his bill, as he was an honest man. This man noticed blood stains on Olschansky's shirt cuff.

Olschansky paid him with a twenty mark gold piece, and this was his undoing.

In the afternoon, the murdered postman was discovered, and the beer man, Gastschenkwirth, reported to the police that twenty marks were paid to him by the man who had not enough money the day before to pay for his food and drink and had asked for credit.

A search was at once instituted for Olschansky, and with the system of registering each lodger with the police by all hotel boarding-house keepers, Olschansky was found, and in his possession were two keys.

I happened to be at the Police Presidium next morning and spoke to Olschansky, who looked more like a caged wolf than a man and had very little to say.

But two weeks later, when found guilty, he had plenty to say and informed the police of the various churches he had robbed, how he obtained keys for the doors, and showed he was a more dangerous criminal than was at first suspected.

After he had been executed, I asked for the keys that had been found in his possession and obtained them. I have found that they will open almost every church door in Germany where they do not use padlocks, and one key seems to be a kind of master key to the spurious Bramah locks.

The handcuff manipulator who imagines that he can go abroad with a few false handcuff keys and make a success has only to give it a trial, and he will find out to his sorrow that an unskilled performer will not be tolerated very long. The Germans, particularly, are like a flame in the pan, a quick flash and then oblivion!

Once in Dortmund, Germany, the landlord of the hotel at which I was stopping came and asked if I would do him a great favor.

A guest who had hired a room by the year was gone for a business trip to Nuremberg and would not be back for several months.

This guest had taken the key of the room with him, and as there happened to be a rush at the hotel, Mr Thrifty Landlord wished to make double revenue by letting this room to a transient guest.

Of course I was not aware of the fact, and to oblige the landlord at his request, I opened the lock of the door. As he wanted a key to the door, I went to a hardware store and purchased a blank key which I intended to cut to fit this lock.

Being an old-fashioned hotel, it had no master keys, and I really went to a lot of trouble to oblige my host.

The next morning I read a three-column article headed: 'Houdini exposed. Buys up all the keys in town, and no wonder he opens all doors.' Then the bright editor told a very interesting story of how he happened to be in the shop and saw Houdini looking over all the blanks and buying several thousands of them; when in reality, I bought one blank, for which I paid five cents (about twenty Pfennige). Ever since that time, I shun hardware shops as I would a pest house.

Opening Sealed Handcuffs
If you wish to have handcuffs sealed, it would be well to try and have a pair rather large so as to slip the hands. You can then easily open the cuff by giving it a sharp blow with the keyhole downwards. Strike the cuff where the hinge and keyhole are on the heel of your shoe or against the floor, and it will spring open. I once used a plate of lead fastened onto drawers at the leg above the knee, sewn in to prevent its slipping away. This was bent to the shape of the leg so that it was not perceived. I struck the cuff where the plate of lead was fixed. This method, however, was rather uncertain.

The Plug Eight Handcuff
The Plug Eight Handcuff is an extraordinarily broad one, used in South Africa during the Boer war, and they say the cuff is used on the Kaffir diamond thieves. No matter how heavy the manacle may be, the locking arrangement is generally the same. This cuff is made by Hiatt of Birmingham, Froggott of Boardsley, and

the one time handcuff maker, Fields. Strange, but almost all of the English cuffs are made in Birmingham or its vicinity.

When open it resembles a double W and when closed, it resembles the figure of eight; after it is locked, you insert a small steel plug into the circular keyhole, and from this steel core of plug, I have named the cuff 'Plug Eight'. In fact I have named every single cuff in the world today. And all of my imitators have taken my 'Tales' and names bodily and without pretense of knowing why the cuff is so called.

The key to the Plug Eight has two teeth at one end: this is the end that unscrews the 'Steel Plug'. After this 'plug' has been removed, you take the other end of the key and insert it into the keyhole and unlock the cuff by turning the key in various directions. Some are female cuffs, which turn from left to right, whilst others are the regulation right to left 'unlocking cuff'. It is very easy to make a master for these cuffs as all work on the same principle.

The easiest cuff to work with is the English Regulation. Having provided yourself with a set of these manacles, you get duplicate keys for the same. With one solitary exception, all these cuffs have spring locks and are manipulated by screwing the key in to open, but they close on pressure with a snap. The exception is what is styled 'Plug Eight'.

For performance: You must adopt the best method suitable to you for concealing your duplicate key. Either in some get-at-able pocket or in a shoe, drapery of cabinet, etc. You may have difficulty in getting handcuffs from your audience, so you must prepare for this emergency by having some of your own secretly 'planted' beforehand by your assistant with some confederates in the audience.

As each come on, you examine the irons and satisfy yourself they are of the regulation pattern as it is from regulation hand-cuffs alone you guarantee to free yourself.

Having examined the cuffs, you allow your committee to lock them on you, all present being satisfied you are securely locked.

You enter your cabinet and, obtaining possession of your duplicate key, you simply unlock cuff and again conceal key. There are, however, some cuffs larger than others, and in this case, you slip one hand from cuff; then it is easy to procure your key and open both.

Moscow Escape

During my engagement at the 'Establishment Yard' in Moscow, Russia, several officers stepped upon the stage to act as a committee, and one of them was very arrogant and would insist on standing in the center of the stage, thereby obstructing the view of the audience. In my politest Russian, I asked him to step aside, but instead of so doing, he demanded how I, a common menial, dared even address him. I honestly did not know what he meant and again asked him to step aside and this time omitting 'Please'. The officer became enraged and planted himself right down in the midst of the footlights, refused to budge, and commanded me to go on with the performance.

By this time, I knew that he was someone of high rank from the way the rest of the folks about bowed, scraped, and fawned to him; so I thought that the best thing I could do was to inform the audience that unless this officer stood aside I would refuse to go on with the show.

The officer only grinned, so I had the cabinet carried down stage so that if the curtain was rung down, it could only come down to the top of my cabinet, and the siege started! There were many officials of high rank in the audience, and soon they started to protest to think that the show had been cut off. Eventually the manager was sent for, and he explained things to me as best he could, but I remained obstinate and insisted that unless this officer stood aside, I would not go on with the show.

It was explained to me that people working for a living, and especially performers, are not looked upon in a favorable light as the majority of Russian men act simply as guides for their acts and generally employ all kinds of women to sing in their troupes, and instead of being paid a salary by the theatrical managers, they have to pay for the privilege of having their troupes work the cabinets. Their cabinets are on the order of the Western wine rooms, only on a very much higher scale.

In Russia, the well-to-do folks come to dine in the cabinets, and if they do not wish to see an act on the stage or have missed a turn, they pay to have the act go through its performance in the cabinet.

The audience in the 'Establishment Yard' was now aroused to a fever pitch, and it was only on my explaining to an officer that in America I was rated as a millionaire, that he profusely apologized to the audience and to me and stepped aside. This officer was the means of obtaining a performance for me at the Palace Kleinmichel where I appeared several times in the presence of the Grand Duke Sergius (who was assassinated several years ago), and we became quite friendly. During one of my entertainments, the Grand Duchess assisted me in the role of Second Sight Artist. All this helped to make a name for me in Russia which will not be forgotten for some time to come. Naturally, this caused a great deal of jealousy amongst the Russian magicians, and one after the other started to run down my performance. Robert Lenz claimed that he did the trunk trick thirty years ago, and because his wife was so much fatter, larger, and more awkward than Madame Houdini, he claimed that his trick was superior. He started in to do a lot of exposing, and one bright morning I arose and found all over the streets of Moscow bright red posters reading, 'Roberta, the Celebrated Exposer, will show you how to escape from all handcuffs, and from all locks.'

I awaited his opening and then saw his show. Of all the false representations and schemes for obtaining money under false pretense, 'Roberta, the Celebrated' took the bun, biscuit and bakeshop.

He did not even know what a handcuff key looked like, and his entire exposure, consisted in removing a rivet from all his manacles, which had been specially prepared for the purpose. The Neck-cuff or Collar is open at the hinge, and the 'false' rivet is shaped like a screw. The false screw or rivet is screwed down tight with a good pair of pliers, so that with the bare hands or fingers no one can unscrew the bolt.

Naturally you can allow anyone to bring along as many locks as they desire, and you can make your escape. All you have to do is to take out your pliers, unscrew the bolt, and close it up again. With this arrangement you can build a large cross or gallows and allow the committee to lock you with as many locks and chains as they wish to bring along, but be sure that they run the chains through the staple or place prepared to hold the locks.

The collar which I invented and used years ago, when being compelled to give two or three performances, was one that fooled even the best magicians in the world. It was made of light metal, and the fake part of it could not be moved either with the fingers or with an instrument. The secret was in the hinge, as I had a steel pin placed in the rivet (which was hollow), and this pin could only be removed by using a strong horseshoe magnet which would pull it up to the top and allow the hinge to open. This method defies detection, and I can honestly recommend it to anyone wishing to make a good set of 'fake' handcuffs or make what is known as a 'Spirit Collar'.

The Spirit Collar
Along with handcuffs and leg irons, there are special types of metal collars made to lock about a person's neck and from which escape is seemingly impossible. The most unusual of these is the 'Spirit Collar' which is made in the shape of an ice pick, with a center rivet which can be examined before and after the escape.

This device is placed about the neck, and the handles are locked, bringing the points of the ice pick close together. These points have small caps on them as protection against their jabbing your neck, and the space between is so slight that it appears impossible to remove the collar without unlocking it. In fact, the lock can be sealed up, but still the collar is removed from the neck, and the seals are found unbroken.

The secret is that a certain part of the neck is very thin. If you put one point of the collar under your chin near your ear, you can force it way into your neck, and you will be able to work the collar from your neck. This is done in a series of stages, carrying the point past the jugular vein, the caps of course preventing injury at that stage.

By gaining as much distance as possible between the points, the escape is facilitated, and you actually accomplish it without tampering with the lock or the collar in any way whatever. This gives the escape the effect of a 'spirit test' presumably accomplished by some unseen aid.

Cologne Police Libel Suit

The police of Germany are very strict in matters of false billing or misrepresenting exhibitions to the public, and so when the Cologne police claimed that I was traveling about misrepresenting, and that my performance was 'swindle', and when Schutzmann Werner Graff published a false story in the *Rheinische Zeitung*, which put me in a very bad light, as a man of honor I could not overlook the insult.

Claiming that I had been slandered, I asked for an apology and a retraction of the false stories which all the press of Germany had copied, but I was simply laughed at for my trouble.

I engaged the best lawyer of Cologne, Herr Rechtsanwalt Dr Schreiber, Louisenstrasse 17, and commenced suit.

The first trial occurred in Cologne, February 19, 1902. I charged that Schutzmann Werner Graff had publicly slandered me, whereupon, as answer, Herr Graff told the judge and jury that he was willing to prove that I was misrepresenting, and that he could chain me so that I could not release myself. I permitted myself to be chained by Herr Transport Police Lott, and to show how easy it was, in the presence of the judge and jury, released myself.

After a four day trial, I won the lawsuit, and the Cologne police were fined and were to apologize to me publicly, 'in the name of the Kaiser'.

Instead of so doing, they took it to the higher court, 'Strafkammer'. At this trial they had specially manufactured a lock which was made by Master mechanic Kroch, which when once locked, could not be opened, not even with the use of the key.

The police asked that I show my ability to open this lock after it had been locked. I accepted the challenge and walked into the room selected by the jury where I could work unhindered, and in four minutes re-entered the court room and handed the judges the prepared lock *unopened*.

Again, I won the lawsuit, and again it was appealed, but this time to the highest court in Germany, 'Oberlandesgericht', and there the learned judges again gave me the verdict from which there was no appeal.

French Letter Cuff

To open the French letter lock get a strong spring, insert it between the two ends of the cuff, which will keep both ends on a tension all the time, and gradually move the letters until you hear a slight click. This you continue to do, until all the letters forming the word or cipher have been found, and then the lock is automatically opened by the pressure of the spring. The finer the workmanship, the harder is the lock to open; but I have never seen any with five or six letters that I have failed to open.

This mention of the French letter cuff reminds me of one of the most exciting and amusing incidents of my continental tour, which I trust will interest my readers. You will recall that I mentioned an eccentric handcuff performer who calls himself Kleppini. This man, with the French letter lock, interrupted my engagement with the Circus Corty Althoff in June, 1902, and brought about one of the most interesting contests that ever fell to my lot. We were touring Holland, when a friend sent me a bill and newspaper clipping, announcing in huge, fat type that Kleppini was about to appear at Circus Sidoli, in Dortmund, Germany, after returning from Holland, where he had defeated the American, Houdini, at his own game. Kleppini further claimed that I had handcuffed him, only to see him escape, while I had met with defeat when handcuffed by him.

This was more than pride could endure. I had a heated argument with my Herr Director, Althoff, who at first refused to allow me to follow up Kleppini and force him to retract; but when I said it was leave of absence or quit for good, he yielded, granted me five days' leave, and I left at once for Dortmund.

Arriving at Essen, a few miles distant from Dortmund, and a town where I had many good friends, I first visited a barber and had him glue a false moustache on my lip, and so fix my hair that I looked like an old man. Then with my small grip filled with 'handcuff-king-defeaters', I was off to Dortmund and the circus, where I found the attendance very light. Kleppini appeared, making his speech in which he claimed to have defeated me. Instantly I was on my feet, crying '*Nicht wahr*', meaning 'Not true'. He asked how I knew this, and I said I was in the know, whereupon he finally offered to wager that he was right. With that I took a flying leap of twenty-two feet downwards to the center of the ring or ménage, as it is called in Germany, and cried, 'You say I am not telling the truth. Well, look! I am Houdini!'

During the controversy which followed I told Kleppini and his manager what honest folk thought of performers and managers who employed misleading and untruthful advertising matter; and I offered five thousand marks if Kleppini would let me handcuff him. Also I offered to escape from his Chinese pillory. He tried to evade the issue, saying he would look me up later, but I insisted that he deposit the money before he started, as I had mine with me.

Herr Director Sidoli refused to make good his advertisements and to back Kleppini for the sum mentioned, so I returned to my seat, and the audience left the circus building in droves, disgusted by the misrepresentations. The next morning, June 18, Herr Reutter, business manager of the circus, came to my hotel with a proposition that I should engage myself one night for a duel with Kleppini, which I refused. Herr Reutter then asked me whether I would handcuff Kleppini if the latter challenged me, and I replied that this I would certainly do. So he begged me to remain one day longer, not allowing anyone to know of my presence in town, however. As I had been working steadily since leaving New York, I was in sad need of rest, so I waited all day in my room, having all meals sent to me. On the morning of June 19, I arose with the lark – to face huge bills announcing, 'Houdini challenged and will appear at the Circus Ceasur Sidoli this evening. Kleppini will allow himself to be handcuffed and will immediately free himself.'

I was more amused than angry. I simply polished my various handcuffs, oiled the mechanism and waited. Kleppini sent for me. I refused to go to him. He called at the hotel. I would not receive him. Manager Reutter then came to me and asked me what cuffs I intended to lock on his star. I said he was at liberty to choose the cuff to be used, and pointed to the twelve cuffs laid out for his inspection. There was one pair of French letter cuffs that caught his fancy, and I permitted him to examine them closely. Reutter then inquired in a peculiar tone, as if feigning indifference: 'What letters or word opens this cuff?'

I perceived his trick at once, and securing his promise that he would not tell Kleppini, I replied, '*Clefs*', which means keys. At the same time I showed him just how to work them. He fell into the trap, and asked me whether he might take these cuffs for Herr Director Sidoli to examine them before the performance, and I told him he was quite at liberty to do so, provided they were not shown to Kleppini. This promise also was given, and he departed, keeping the cuffs in his possession four hours. Of course I knew that during this time Kleppini was familiarizing himself with the cuffs, but I still had a trick up my own sleeve.

That night at the circus I occupied a box seat, and when Kleppini threw out his daring challenge, I entered the ring with my bag of cuffs. I said that I had no objection to his advertising his willingness to let me handcuff him, but I did object to his stating he could get out until he had made good. The audience was with me, and I told him to take his choice of the twelve cuffs. As I anticipated, he sprang like a tiger on the French letter cuff. He had taken them closed, and ran with feverish haste into his cabinet.

He remained within about three minutes, whereupon I cried: 'Ladies and gentlemen, do not let him tell you that the cuffs have been locked. They are open. He will return and say he opened them.' This brought him out of his cabinet waving the cuffs like a crazy man, and crying, 'I will open these cuffs. I challenge Houdini to lock them on me. I'll show him that it is us Germans who lead the world.'

As he had tried the cuffs in the cabinet, he was positive that he could beat them. And I was just as positive that the opposite conditions would prevail. He now started to goad me into locking them on quickly, pressing me all over the circus. So violent were my efforts, that my heart beat like a trip hammer, and my face turned pale from exertion. From this Kleppini gathered that I thought myself even then defeated. So he walked to the centre of the ring, with the handcuffs locked upon him, and cried: 'After I open these handcuffs, I will allow Madame Kleppini to open them. She is very clever in this branch of work, and she will open them in five seconds.'

I smiled grimly and took the floor. 'Ladies and gentlemen, you can all go home. I do not lock a cuff on a man merely to let him escape. If he tries this cuff until doomsday, he cannot open it. To prove this, though the regular closing time of the circus is 10.30, I will allow him to remain here until 2.30.'

He went into his cabinet at nine o'clock. When the big ballet feature came on at 9.30, he was not ready. At 11, almost the entire audience had gone, and Kleppini was still in his cabinet. Herr Director Sidoli became enraged, and instructed his servants to 'out with Kleppini', and they lifted the cabinet up bodily and threw it over. Kleppini ran like a hunted animal into the manager's dressing room. The rest of the show might have gone on, but the audience rose as a man and went out.

At midnight, by which time I had left my place in the box, and was standing guard over the dressing room door, I permitted Madame Kleppini to join her husband, at his request. About one o'clock the manager asked Kleppini if he would give up, and Kleppini begged me to enter the room and release him, which I refused to do without witnesses. We then sent for the Herr Director Sidoli, Herr Reutter, and a reporter. At last Kleppini said he had the word '*Clefs*', and I laughed.

'You are wrong. If you want to know the word which opens the lock, it is just what you are – "fraud".' And with this I grabbed his hands, quickly turned the letters till they spelled 'fraud', and as they fell into their respective places he was freed.

The locks, you see, were changeable, and it required only a short moment for me to change the word. When he went into the cabinet, he tried the cuff, and it responded to the word '*Clefs*'. While locking them on him, I changed the word to 'fraud', and he, even with his eagle eye, failed to recognize that he had been trapped.

The next day, however, being a boastful man, and unwilling to acknowledge defeat, he actually circulated bills stating that he had defeated Houdini and won five thousand marks; but the newspapers guyed him unmercifully, and published the true facts.

Miracle-Mongers and Their Methods

'All wonder,' said Samuel Johnson, 'is the effect of novelty on ignorance.' Yet we are so created that without something to wonder at we should find life scarcely worth living. That fact does not make ignorance bliss, or make it 'folly to be wise'. For the wisest man never gets beyond the reach of novelty, nor can ever make it his boast that there is nothing he is ignorant of; on the contrary, the wiser he becomes the more clearly he sees how much there is of which he remains in ignorance. The more he knows, the more he will find to wonder at.

My professional life has been a constant record of disillusion, and many things that seem wonderful to most men are the everyday commonplaces of my business. But I have never been without some seeming marvel to pique my curiosity and challenge my investigation. In this book I have set down some of the stories of strange folk and unusual performers that I have gathered in many years of such research.

Much has been written about the feats of miracle-mongers, and not a little in the way of explaining them. Chaucer was by no means the first to turn shrewd eyes upon wonder-workers and show the clay feet of these popular idols. And since his time innumerable marvels, held to be supernatural, have been exposed for the tricks they were. Yet today, if a mystifier lacks the ingenuity to invent a new and startling stunt, he can safely fall back upon a trick that has been the favorite of press-agents the world over in all ages. He can imitate the Hindu fakir who, having thrown a rope high into the air, has a boy climb it until he is lost to view. He can even have the feat photographed. The camera will click; nothing will appear on the developed film; and this, the performer will glibly explain, 'proves' that the whole company of onlookers was hypnotized! And he can be certain of a very profitable following to defend and advertise him.

So I do not feel that I need to apologize for adding another volume to the shelves of works dealing with the marvels of the miracle-mongers. My business has given me an intimate knowledge of stage illusions, together with many years of experience among show people of all types. My familiarity with the former, and what I have learned of the psychology of the latter, have placed me at a certain advantage in uncovering the natural explanation of feats that to the ignorant have seemed supernatural. And even if my readers are too well informed to be interested in my descriptions of the methods of the various performers who have seemed to me worthy of attention in these pages, I hope they will find some amusement in following the fortunes and misfortunes of all manner of strange folk who once bewildered the wise men of their day. If I have accomplished that much, I shall feel amply repaid for my labor.

Fire-Eaters

The yellow thread of exposure seems to be inextricably woven into all fabrics whose strength is secrecy, and experience proves that it is much easier to become fireproof than to become exposure proof. It is still an open question, however, as to what extent exposure really injures a performer. Exposure of the secrets of the fire-eaters, for instance, dates back almost to the beginning of the art itself. The priests were exposed, Richardson was exposed, Powell was exposed and so on down the line; but the business continued to prosper, the really clever performers drew quite fashionable audiences for a long time, and it was probably the demand for a higher form of entertainment, resulting from a refinement of the public taste, rather than the result of the many exposures, that finally relegated the fire-eaters to the haunts of the proletariat.

How the early priests came into possession of these secrets does not appear, and if there were ever any records of this kind the Church would hardly allow them to become public. That they used practically the same system which has been adopted by all their followers is amply proved by the fact that after trial by ordeal had been abolished Albertus Magnus, in his work *De Mirabilibus Mundi*, at the end of his book *De Secretis Mulierum*, Amstelod, 1702, made public the underlying principles of heat resistance; namely, the use of certain compounds which render the exposed parts to a more or less extent impervious to heat. Many different formulas have been discovered which accomplish the purpose, but the principle remains unchanged. The formula set down by Albertus Magnus was probably the first ever made public: the following translation of it is from *The London Mirror*:

> Take juice of marshmallow, and white of egg, flea-bane seeds, and lime; powder them and mix juice of radish with the white of egg; mix all thoroughly and with this composition anoint

your body or hand and allow it to dry and afterwards anoint it again, and after this you may boldly take up hot iron without hurt.

'Such a paste,' says the correspondent to *The Mirror*, 'would indeed be very visible.'

Another early formula is given in the 1763 edition of *Hocus Pocus*. Examination of the different editions of this book in my library discloses the fact that there are no fire formulas in the second edition, 1635, which is the earliest I have (first editions are very rare and there is only one record of a sale of that edition at auction). From the fact that this formula was published during the time that Powell was appearing in England, I gather that that circumstance may account for its addition to the book. It does not appear in the German or Dutch editions. The following is an exact copy,

How To Walk on a Hot Iron Bar Without Any Danger of Scalding or Burning.

Take half an ounce of samphire, dissolve it in two ounces of aquaevitae, add to it one ounce of quicksilver, one ounce of liquid storax, which is the droppings of myrrh and hinders the camphire from firing; take also two ounces of hematitus, a red stone to be had at the druggist's, and when you buy it let them beat it to powder in their great mortar, for it is so very hard that it cannot be done in a small one; put this to the afore-mentioned composition, and when you intend to walk on the bar you must anoint your feet well therewith, and you may walk over without danger: by this you may wash your hands in boiling lead.

This was the secret modus operandi made use of by Richardson, the first notably successful fire artist to appear in Europe, and it was disclosed by his servant.*

Hone's *Table Book*, London, 1827, page 315, gives Richardson's method as follows,

> It consisted only in rubbing the hands and thoroughly washing the mouth, lips, tongue, teeth and other parts which were to touch the fire, with pure spirits of sulphur. This burns and cauterizes the epidermis or upper skin, till it becomes as hard and thick as leather, and each time the experiment is tried it becomes still easier. But if, after it has been very often repeated the upper skin should grow so callous and hard as to become troublesome, washing the parts affected with very warm water, or hot wine, will bring away all the shriveled or parched epidermis. The flesh, however, will continue tender and unfit for such business till it has been frequently rubbed over with the same spirit.
>
> This preparation may be rendered much stronger and more efficacious by mixing equal quantities of spirit of sulphur, sal ammoniac, essence of rosemary and juice of onions. The bad effects which frequently swallowing red-hot coals, melted sealing wax, rosin, brimstone and other calcined and inflammable matter, might have had upon his stomach were prevented by drinking plentifully of warm water and oil, as soon as he left the company, till he had vomited it all up again.

This anecdote was communicated to the author of the *Journal des Savants* by Mr Panthot, Doctor of Physics and Member of the College at Lyons. It appeared at the time Powell was showing his

* Such disloyalty in trusted servants is one of the most disheartening things that can happen to a public performer. But it must not be thought that I say this out of personal experience: for in the many years that I have been before the public my secret methods have been steadily shielded by the strict integrity of my assistants, most of whom have been with me for years. Only one man ever betrayed my confidence, and that only in a minor matter. But then, so far as I know, I am the only performer who ever pledged his assistants to secrecy, honor and allegiance under a notarial oath.

fire-eating stunts in London, and the correspondent naively added,

> Whether Mr Powell will take it kindly of me thus to have published his secret I cannot tell; but as he now begins to drop into years, has no children that I know of and may die suddenly, or without making a will, I think it a great pity so genteel an occupation should become one of the *artes perditae*, as possibly it may, if proper care is not taken, and therefore hope, after this information, some true-hearted Englishman will take it up again, for the honor of his country, when he reads in the newspapers, 'Yesterday, died, much lamented, the famous Mr Powell. He was the best, if not the only, fire-eater in the world, and it is greatly to be feared that his art is dead with him.'

After a couple of columns more in a similar strain, the correspondent signs himself Philopyraphagus Ashburniensis.

In his *History of Inventions*, Vol. III, page 272, 1817 edition, Beckmann thus describes the process:

> The deception of breathing out flames, which at present excites, in a particular manner, the astonishment of the ignorant, is very ancient. When the slaves in Sicily, about a century and a half before our era, made a formidable insurrection, and avenged themselves in a cruel manner, for the severities which they had suffered, there was amongst them a Syrian named Eunus – a man of great craft and courage; who having passed through many scenes of life, had become acquainted with a variety of arts. He pretended to have immediate communication with the gods; was the oracle and leader of his fellow slaves; and, as is usual on such occasions confirmed his divine mission by miracles. When heated by enthusiasm and desirous of inspiring his followers with courage, he breathed flames or sparks among them from his mouth while he was addressing

them. We are told by historians that for this purpose he pierced a nut shell at both ends, and, having filled it with some burning substance, put it into his mouth and breathed through it. This deception, at present, is performed much better. The juggler rolls together some flax or hemp, so as to form a ball about the size of a walnut; sets it on fire; and suffers it to burn until it is nearly consumed; he then rolls round it, while burning, some more flax; and by these means the fire may be retained in it for a long time. When he wishes to exhibit he slips the ball unperceived into his mouth, and breathes through it; which again revives the fire, so that a number of weak sparks proceed from it; and the performer sustains no hurt, provided he inspire the air not through the mouth, but the nostrils. By this art the Rabbi Bar-Cocheba, in the reign of the Emperor Hadrian, made the credulous Jews believe that he was the hoped-for Messiah; and two centuries after, the Emperor Constantius was thrown into great terror when Valentinian informed him that he had seen one of the bodyguards breathing out fire and flames in the evening.

Since Beckmann wrote, the method of producing smoke and sparks from the mouth has been still further improved. The fire can now be produced in various ways. One way is by the use of a piece of thick cotton string which has been soaked in a solution of nitre and then thoroughly dried. This string, when once lighted, burns very slowly and a piece one inch long is sufficient for the purpose. Some performers prefer a small piece of punk, as it requires no preparation. Still others use tinder made by burning linen rags, as our forefathers used to do. This will not flame, but merely smolders until the breath blows it into a glow. The tinder is made by charring linen rags, that is, burning them to a crisp, but stopping the combustion before they are reduced to ashes.

Flames from the lips may be produced by holding in the mouth a sponge saturated with the purest gasoline. When the breath is exhaled sharply it can be lighted from a torch or a candle. Closing the lips firmly will extinguish the flame. A wad of oakum will give better results than the sponge.

Natural gas is produced as simply. A T-shaped gas pipe has three or four gas tips on the cross-piece. The long end is placed in the mouth, which already holds concealed a sponge, or preferably a ball of oakum, saturated with pure gasoline. Blowing through the pipe will force the gas through the tips, where it can be ignited with a match. It will burn as long as the breath lasts.

In a London periodical, *The Terrific Record*, appears a reprint from the *Mercure de France*, giving an account of experiments in Naples which led to the discovery of the means by which jugglers have appeared to be incombustible. They first gradually habituate the skin, the mouth, throat and stomach to great degrees of heat, then they rub the skin with hard soap. The tongue is also covered with hard soap and over that a layer of powdered sugar. By this means an investigating professor was enabled to reproduce the wonders which had puzzled many scientists.

The investigating professor in all probability, was Professor Sementini, who experimented with Lionetto. I find an account of Sementini's discoveries in an old newspaper clipping, the name and date of which have unfortunately been lost:

Sementini's efforts, after performing several experiments upon himself, were finally crowned with success. He found that by friction with sulphuric acid diluted with water, the skin might be made insensible to the action of the heat of red-hot iron; a solution of alum, evaporated till it became spongy, appeared to be more effectual in these frictions. After having rubbed the parts which were thus rendered in some degree insensible, with hard soap, he discovered, on the application of hot iron, that their insensibility was increased. He then determined on again rubbing the parts with soap, and after that found that the hot iron not only occasioned no pain but that it actually did not burn the hair.

Being thus far satisfied, the Professor applied hard soap to his tongue until it became insensible to the heat of the iron; and having placed an ointment composed of soap mixed with a solution of alum upon it, burning oil did not burn it; while the oil remained on the tongue a slight hissing was heard, similar to that of hot iron when thrust into water; the oil soon cooled and might then be swallowed without danger.

Several scientific men have since repeated the experiments of Professor Sementini, but we would not recommend any except professionals to try the experiments.

Liquid storax is now used to anoint the tongue when red-hot irons are to be placed in the mouth. It is claimed that with this alone a red-hot poker can be licked until it is cold.

Another formula is given by Griffin, as follows: one bar ivory soap, cut fine, one pound of brown sugar, two ounces liquid storax (not the gum). Dissolve in hot water and add a wineglassful of carbolic acid. This is rubbed on all parts liable to come in contact with the hot articles. After anointing the mouth with this solution, rinse with strong vinegar.

No performer should attempt to bite off red-hot iron unless he has a good set of teeth. A piece of hoop iron may be prepared by bending it back and forth at a point about one inch from the end, until the fragment is nearly broken off, or by cutting nearly through it with a cold chisel. When the iron has been heated red-hot, the prepared end is taken between the teeth, and a couple of bends will complete the break. The piece which drops from the teeth into a dish of water will make a puff of steam and a hissing sound, which will demonstrate that it is still very hot.

The mystery of the burning cage, in which the Fire King remains while a steak is thoroughly cooked, is explained by Barnello as follows:

Have a large iron cage constructed about four feet by six feet, the bottom made of heavy sheet iron. The cage should stand on iron legs or horses. Wrap each of the bars of the cage with cotton batting saturated with oil. Now take a raw beefsteak in your hand and enter the cage, which is now set on fire. Remain in the cage until the fire has burned out, then issue from the cage with the steak burned to a crisp.

Explanation, on entering the cage the performer places the steak on a large iron hook which is fastened in one of the upper corners. The dress worn is of asbestos cloth with a hood that completely covers the head and neck. There is a small hole over the mouth through which he breathes.

As soon as the fire starts the smoke and flames completely hide the performer from the spectators, and he immediately lies down on the bottom of the cage, placing the mouth over one of the small air holes in the floor of the same.

Heat always goes up and will soon cook the steak.

I deduce from the above that the performer arises and recovers the steak when the fire slackens but while there is still sufficient flame and smoke to mask his action.

It is obvious that the above explanation covers the baker's oven mystery as well. In the case of the oven, however, the inmate is concealed from start to finish, and this gives him much greater latitude for his actions. M Chabert made the oven the big feature of his programme and succeeded in puzzling many of the best informed scientists of his day.

Eating coals of fire has always been one of the sensational feats of the fire kings, as it is quite generally known that charcoal burns with an extremely intense heat. This fervent lunch, however, like many of the feasts of the fire kings, is produced by trick methods. Mixed with the charcoal in the brazier are a few coals of soft white pine, which when burnt look exactly like charcoal. These will not burn the mouth as charcoal will. They should be picked up with a fork which will penetrate the pine coals, but not the charcoal, the latter being brittle.

Another method of eating burning coals employs small balls of burned cotton in a dish of burning alcohol. When lifted on the fork these have the appearance of charcoal, but are harmless if the mouth be immediately closed, so that the flame is extinguished.

In all feats of fire-eating it should be noted that the head is thrown well back, so that the flame may pass out of the open mouth instead of up into the roof, as it would if the head were held naturally.

To drink burning oil set fire to a small quantity of kerosene in a ladle. Into this dip an iron spoon and bring it up to all appearance, filled with burning oil, though in reality the spoon is merely wet with the oil. It is carried blazing to the mouth, where it is tipped, as if to pour the oil into the mouth, just as a puff breath blows out all the flame. The process is continued until all the oil in the ladle has been consumed; then the ladle is turned bottom up, in order to show that all the oil has been drunk.

A method of drinking what seems to be molten lead is given in the Chambers' *Book of Days*, 1863, Vol. II, page 278.

The performer taking an iron spoon, holds it up to the spectators, to show that it is empty; then, dipping it into a pot containing melted lead, he again shows it to the spectators full of the molten metal; then, after putting the spoon in his mouth, he once more shows it to be empty; and after compressing his lips, with a look expressive of pain, he, in a few moments, ejects from his mouth a piece of lead impressed with the exact form of his teeth. Ask a spectator what he saw, and he will say that the performer took a spoonful of molten lead, placed it in his mouth, and soon afterwards showed it in a solid state, bearing the exact form and impression of his teeth. If deception be insinuated, the spectator will say, 'No! Having the evidence of my senses, I cannot be deceived; if it had been a matter of opinion I might, but seeing, you know, is believing.' Now the piece of lead, cast from a plaster mould of the performer's teeth, has probably officiated in a thousand previous performances, and is placed in the mouth between the gum and the cheek, just before the trick commences. The spoon is made with a hollow handle containing quicksilver, which, by a simple motion, can be let run into the bowl, or back again into the handle at will.

The spoon is first shown with the quicksilver concealed in the handle, the bowl is then dipped just within the rim of the pot containing the molten lead, but not into the lead itself, and, at the same instant the quicksilver is allowed to run into the bowl. The spoon is then shown with the quicksilver (which the audience takes to be the melted lead) in the bowl, and when placed in the mouth, the quicksilver is again allowed to run into the handle.

The performer, in fact, takes a spoonful of nothing, and soon after exhibits the lead bearing the impression of the teeth.

Molten lead, for fire-eating purposes, is made as follows:

Bismuth	5 oz.
Lead	3 oz.
Block tin	2 oz.

Melt these together. When the metal has cooled, a piece the size of a silver quarter can be melted and taken into the mouth and held there until it hardens. This alloy will melt in boiling water. Robert-Houdin calls it Arcet's metal, but I cannot find the name elsewhere.

The eating of burning brimstone is an entirely fake perform-ance. A number of small pieces of brimstone are shown, and then wrapped in cotton which has been saturated with a half-and-half mixture of kerosene and gasoline, the surplus oil having been squeezed out so there shall be no drip. When these are lighted they may be held in the palm of any hand which has been anointed with one of the fire mixtures described in this chapter. Then throw back the head, place the burning ball in the mouth, and a freshly extinguished candle can be lighted from the flame. Close the lips firmly, which will extinguish the flame, then chew and pretend to swallow the brimstone, which can afterwards be removed under cover of a handkerchief.

Observe that the brimstone has not been burned at all, and that the cotton protects the teeth. To add to the effect, a small piece of brimstone may be dropped into the furnace, a very small piece will suffice to convince all that it is the genuine article that is being eaten.

To cause the face to appear in a mass of flame make use of the following: mix together thoroughly petroleum, lard, mutton tallow and quick lime. Distill this over a charcoal fire, and the liquid which results can be burned on the face without harm.*

To set paper on fire by blowing upon it, small pieces of wet phosphorus are taken into the mouth, and a sheet of tissue paper is held about a foot from the lips. While the paper is being blown upon, the phosphorus is ejected on it, although this passes unnoticed by the spectators, and as soon as the continued blowing has dried the phosphorus it will ignite the paper.

Drinking boiling liquor is accomplished by using a cup with a false bottom, under which the liquor is retained.

A solution of spermaceti in sulphuric ether tinged with alkanet root, which solidifies fifty degrees Fahrenheit, and melts and boils with the heat of the hand, is described in Beckmann's *History of Inventions*, Vol. II., page 121.

Dennison's No. 2 sealing wax may be melted in the flame of a candle and, while still blazing, dropped upon the tongue without causing a burn, as the moisture of the tongue instantly cools it. Care must be used, however, that none touches the hands or

* Barnello's *Red Demon*.

lips. It can be chewed, and apparently swallowed, but removed in the handkerchief while wiping the lips.

The above is the method practiced by all the fire-eaters, and absolutely no preparation is necessary except that the tongue must be well moistened with saliva.

Barnello once said, 'A person wishing to become a fire-eater must make up his or her mind to suffer a little at first from burns, as there is no one who works at the business but that gets burns either from carelessness or from accident.'

This is verified by the following, which I clip from *The London Globe* of August 11th, 1880,

Accident to a fire-eater. A correspondent telegraphs: A terrible scene was witnessed in the market place, Leighton Buzzard, yesterday. A travelling Negro fire eater was performing on a stand, licking red-hot iron, bending heated pokers with his naked foot, burning tow in his mouth, and the like. At last he filled his mouth with benzolene, saying that he would burn it as he allowed it to escape. He had no sooner applied a lighted match to his lips than the whole mouthful of spirit took fire and before it was consumed the man was burned in a frightful manner, the blazing spirit running all over his face, neck and chest as he dashed from his stand and raced about like a madman among the assembled crowd, tearing his clothing from him and howling in most intense agony. A portion of the spirit was swallowed and the inside of his mouth was also terribly burnt. He was taken into a chemist's shop and oils were administered and applied, but afterwards in agonizing frenzy he escaped in a state almost of nudity from a lodging house and was captured by the police and taken to the workhouse infirmary, where he remains in a dreadful condition.

Remember! Always have a large blanket at hand to smother flames in burning clothing – also a bucket of water and a quantity of sand. A siphon of carbonic water is an excellent fire extinguisher.

The gas of gasoline is heavier than air, so a container should never be held *above* a flame. Keep kerosene and gasoline containers well corked and at a distance from fire.

Never inhale breath while performing with fire. *Flame drawn into the lungs is fatal to life*.

So much for the entertaining side of the art. There are, however, some further scientific principles so interesting that I reserve them for another chapter.

Sword-Swallowers

It has sometimes been noted in the foregoing pages, that fire-eaters, finding it difficult to invent new effects in their own sphere, have strayed into other fields of endeavor in order to amplify their programmes. Thus we find them resorting to the allied arts of poison eating, sword-swallowing and the stunts of the so-called Human Ostrich.

In this connection, I consider it not out of place for me to include a description of a number of those who have, either through unusual gifts of nature or through clever artifice, seemingly submitted to tests which we have been taught to believe were far and away beyond the outposts of human endurance. By the introduction of these thrills each notable newcomer has endeavored to go his predecessors one better, and the issue of challenges to all comers to match these startling effects has been by no means infrequent, but I fail to discover a single acceptance of such a challenge.

To accomplish the sword-swallowing feat, it is only necessary to overcome the nausea that results from the metal's touching the mucous membrane of the pharynx, for there is an unobstructed passage, large enough to accommodate several of the thin blades used, from the mouth to the bottom of the stomach. This passage is not straight, but the passing of the sword straightens it. Some throats are more sensitive than others, but practice will soon accustom any throat to the passage of the blade. When a sword with a sharp point is used the performer secretly slips a rubber cap over the point to guard against accident.

It is said that the medical fraternity first learned of the possibility of overcoming the sensitiveness of the pharynx by investigating the methods of the sword-swallowers.

Cliquot, who was one of the most prominent sword-swallowers of his time, finally 'reformed' and is now a music hall agent in England. *The Strand Magazine* (1896) has this to say of Cliquot and his art,

The Chevalier Cliquot (these fellows *must* have titles) in the act of swallowing the major part of a cavalry sword twenty-two inches long. Cliquot, whose name suggests the swallowing of something much more grateful and comforting than steel swords, is a French Canadian by birth, and has been the admitted chief in his profession for more than eighteen years. He ran away from his home in Quebec at an early age, and joined a traveling circus bound for South America. On seeing an arrant old humbug swallow a small machete, in Buenos Aires, the boy took a fancy to the performance, and approached the old humbug aforesaid with the view of being taught the business. Not having any money, however, wherewith to pay the necessary premium, the overtures of the would-be apprentice were repulsed; whereupon he set about experimenting with his own esophagus with a piece of silver wire.

To say the preliminary training for this sort of thing is painful, is to state the fact most moderately; and even when stern purpose has triumphed over the laws of anatomy, terrible danger still remains.

On one occasion having swallowed a sword, and then bent his body in different directions, as an adventurous sensation, Cliquot found that the weapon also had bent to a sharp angle; and quick as thought, realizing his own position as well as that of the sword, he whipped it out, tearing his throat in a dreadful manner. Plainly, had the upper part of the weapon become detached, the sword-swallower's career must infallibly have come to an untimely end. Again, in New York, when swallowing fourteen nine-inch bayonet swords at once, Cliquot had the misfortune to have a too skeptical audience, one of whom, a medical man who ought to have known better, rushed forward and impulsively dragged out the whole bunch, inflicting such injuries upon this peculiar entertainer as to endanger his life, and incapacitate him for months.

In one of his acts Cliquot swallows a real bayonet sword, weighted with a crossbar, and two eighteen-pound dumbbells.

In order to vary this performance, the sword-swallower allows only a part of the weapon to pass into his body, the remainder being 'kicked' down by the recoil of a rifle, which is fixed to a spike in the centre of the bar, and fired by the performer's sister.

The last act in this extraordinary performance is the swallowing of a gold watch. As a rule, Cliquot borrows one, but as no timepiece was forthcoming at the private exhibition where I saw him, he proceeded to lower his own big chronometer into his esophagus by a slender gold chain. Many of the most eminent physicians and surgeons in this country immediately rushed forward with various instruments, and the privileged few took turns in listening for the ticking of the watch inside the performer's body. 'Poor, outraged nature is biding her time,' remarked one physician, 'but mark me, she will have a terrible revenge sooner or later!'

Eaters of glass, tacks, pebbles, and like objects, actually swallow these seemingly impossible things, and disgorge them after the performance is over. That the disgorging is not always successful is evidenced by the hospital records of many surgical operations on performers of this class, when quantities of solid matter are found lodged in the stomach.

Delno Fritz was not only an excellent sword-swallower, but a good showman as well. The last time I saw him he was working the 'halls' in England. I hope he saved his money, for he was a clean man with a clean reputation, and, I can truly say, he was a master in his manner of indulging his appetite for the cold steel.

Deodota, an Italian Magician, was also a sword-swallower of more than average ability. He succumbed to the lure of commercialism finally, and is now in the jewelry business in the 'downtown district' of New York City.

Sword-swallowing may be harmlessly imitated by the use of a fake sword with a telescopic blade, which slides into the handle. Vosin, the Paris manufacturer of magical apparatus, made swords of this type, but they were generally used in theatrical enchant-ment scenes, and it is very doubtful if they were ever used by professional swallowers.

It is quite probable that the swords now most generally used by the profession, which are cut from one piece of metal – handle and all were introduced to show that they were free from any telescoping device. Swords of this type are quite thin, less than one-eighth of an inch thick, and four or five of them can be swallowed at once. Slowly withdrawing them one at a time, and throwing them on the stage in different directions, makes an effective display.

A small, but strong, electric light bulb attached to the end of a cane, is a very effective piece of apparatus for sword-swallowers, as on a darkened stage, the passage of the light down the throat and into the stomach can be plainly seen by the audience. The medical profession now make use of this idea.

By apparently swallowing sharp razors, a dime-museum performer, whose name I do not recall, gave a variation to the sword-swallowing stunt. This was in the later days, and the act was partly fake and partly genuine. That is to say, the swallowing was fair enough, but the sharp razors, after being tested by cutting hairs, etc., were exchanged for dull duplicates, in a manner that, in better hands, might have been effective. This chap belonged to the great army of unconscious exposers, and the 'switch' was quite apparent to all save the most careless observers.

His apparatus consisted of a fancy rack on which three sharp razors were displayed, and a large bandana handkerchief, in which there were several pockets of the size to hold a razor, the three dull razors being loaded in this. After testing the edge of the sharp razors, he pretended to wipe them, one by one, with the handkerchief, and under cover of this he made the 'switch' for the dull ones, which he proceeded to swallow in the ortho-`dox fashion. His work was crude, and the crowd was inclined to poke fun at him.

I have seen one of these performers on the street, in London, swallow a borrowed umbrella, after carefully wiping the ferrule, and then return it to its owner only slightly dampened from its unusual journey. A borrowed watch was swallowed by the same performer, and while one end of the chain hung from the lips, the incredulous onlookers were invited to place their ears against his chest and listen to the ticking of the watch, which had passed as far into the esophagus as the chain would allow.

The following anecdote from the *Carlisle Journal*, shows that playing with sword-swallowing is about as dangerous as playing with fire.

Distressing Occurrence

On Monday evening last, a man named William Dempster, a juggler of inferior dexterity while exhibiting his tricks in a public house in Botchergate, kept by a person named Purdy, actually accomplished the sad reality of one of those feats, with the semblance only of which he intended to amuse his audience. Having introduced into his throat a common table knife which he was intending to swallow, he accidentally slipped his hold, and the knife passed into his stomach. An alarm was immediately given, and surgical aid procured, but the knife had passed beyond the reach of instruments, and now remains in his stomach. He has since been attended by most of the medical gentlemen of this city; and we understand that no very alarming symptoms have yet appeared, and that it is possible he may exist a considerable time, even in this awkward state.

His sufferings at first were very severe, but he is now, when not in motion, comparatively easy. The knife is nine and a half inches long, one inch broad in the blade, round pointed, and a handle of bone, and may generally be distinctly felt by applying the finger to the unfortunate man's belly; but occasionally, however, from change of its situation it is not perceptible. A brief notice of the analogous case of John Cumming, an American sailor, may not be unacceptable to our readers. About the year 1799, he, in imitation of some jugglers whose exhibition he had then witnessed, in an hour of intoxication, swallowed four clasp knives such as sailors commonly use; all of which passed from him in a few days without much inconvenience. Six years afterward, he swallowed *fourteen* knives of different sizes; by these, however, he was much disordered, but recovered; and again, in a paroxysm of intoxication, he actually swallowed *seventeen*, of the effects of which he died in March, 1809. On dissection, fourteen knife blades were found remaining in his stomach, and the back spring of one penetrating through the bowel, seemed the immediate cause of his death.

Several women have adopted the profession of sword-swallowing, and some have won much more than a passing fame. Notable among these is Mlle Edith Clifford, who is, perhaps, the most generously endowed. Possessed of more than ordinary personal charms, a refined taste for dressing both herself and her stage, and an unswerving devotion to her art, she has perfected an act that has found favor even in the Royal Courts of Europe.

Mlle Clifford was born in London in 1884 and began swallowing the blades when only fifteen years of age. During the foreign tour of the Barnum & Bailey show she joined that organization in Vienna, 1901, and remained with it for five years, and now, after eighteen years of service, she stands well up among the stars. She has swallowed a twenty-six inch blade, but the physicians advise her not to indulge her appetite for such luxuries often, as it is quite dangerous. Blades of eighteen or twenty inches give her no trouble whatever.

In the spring of 1919, I visited the Ringling Brothers, and the Barnum & Bailey Show especially to witness Mlle Clifford's act. In addition to swallowing the customary swords and sabers she introduced such novelties as a specially constructed razor; with a blade five or six times the usual length, a pair of scissors of unusual size, a saw which is two and a half inches wide at the broadest point, with ugly looking teeth, although somewhat rounded at the points, and several other items quite unknown to the bill of fare of ordinary mortals. A set of ten thin blades slip easily down her throat and are removed one at a time.

The sensation of her act is reached when the point of a bayonet, twenty-three and a half inches long, fastened to the breech of a cannon, is placed in her mouth and the piece discharged; the recoil driving the bayonet suddenly down her throat. The gun is loaded with a ten gauge cannon shell.

Mlle Clifford's handsomely arranged stage occupied the place of honor in the section devoted to freaks and specialties.

Cliquot told me that Delno Fritz was his pupil, and Mlle Clifford claims to be a pupil of Fritz.

Deserving of honorable mention also is a native of Berlin, who bills herself as Victorina. This lady is able to swallow a dozen sharp-bladed swords at once. Of Victorina, *The Boston Herald* of December 28th, 1902, said,

By long practice she has accustomed herself to swallow swords, daggers, bayonets, walking sticks, rods, and other dangerous articles.

Her throat and food passages have become so expansive that she can swallow three long swords almost up to the hilts, and can accommodate a dozen shorter blades.

This woman is enabled to bend a blade after swallowing it. By moving her head back and forth she may even twist instruments in her throat. To bend the body after one has swallowed a sword is a dangerous feat, even for a professional swallower. There is a possibility of severing some of the ligaments of the throat or else large arteries or veins. Victorina has already had several narrow escapes.

On one occasion, while sword-swallowing before a Boston audience, a sword pierced a vein in her throat. The blade was half-way down, but instead of immediately drawing it forth, she thrust it farther. She was laid up in a hospital for three months after this performance.

In Chicago she had a still narrower escape. One day while performing at a museum on Clark Street, Victorina passed a long thin dagger down her throat. In withdrawing it, the blade snapped in two, leaving the pointed portion some distance in the passage. The woman nearly fainted when she realized what had occurred, but, by a masterful effort, controlled her feelings. Dropping the hilt of the dagger on the floor, she leaned forward, and placing her finger and thumb down her throat, just succeeded in catching the end of the blade. Had it gone down an eighth of an inch farther her death would have been certain.

Defiers of Poisonous Reptiles

About twenty-two years ago, during one of my many engage-ments at Kohl and Middleton's, Chicago, there appeared at the same house a marvelous 'rattlesnake-poison defier' named Thardo. I watched her act with deep interest for a number of weeks, never missing a single performance. For the simple reason that I worked within twelve feet from her, my statement that there was absolutely no fake attached to her startling performance can be taken in all seriousness, as the details are still fresh in my mind.

Thardo was a woman of exceptional beauty, both of form and feature, a fluent speaker and a fearless enthusiast in her devotion to her art. She would allow herself to be repeatedly bitten by rattlesnakes and received no harm excepting the ordinary pain of the wound. After years of investigation I have come to the belief that this immunity was the result of an absolutely empty stomach, into which a large quantity of milk was taken shortly after the wound was inflicted, the theory being that the virus acts directly on the contents of the stomach, changing it to a deadly poison.

It was Thardo's custom to give weekly demonstrations of this power, to which the medical profession were invited, and on these occasions she was invariably greeted with a packed house. When the moment of the supreme test came, an awed silence obtained; for the thrill of seeing the serpent flash up and strike possessed a positive fascination for her audiences. Her bare arms and shoulders presented a tempting target for the death-dealing reptile whose anger she had aroused. As soon as he had buried his fangs in her expectant flesh, she would coolly tear him from the wound and allow one of the physicians present to extract a portion of the venom and inject it into a rabbit, with the result that the poor creature would almost instantly go into convulsions and would soon die in great agony.

Another rattlesnake defier is a resident of San Antonio, Texas. Her name is Learn, and she once told me that she was the preceptor of Thardo. This lady deals in live rattlesnakes and their by-products – rattlesnake skin, which is used for fancy bags and purses; rattlesnake oil, which is highly esteemed in some quarters as a specific for rheumatism; and the venom, which has a pharmaceutical value.

She employs a number of men as snake trappers. Their usual technique is to pin the rattler to the ground by means of a forked stick thrust dexterously over his neck, after which he is conveyed into a bag made for the purpose. Probably the cleverest of her trappers is a Mexican who has a faculty of catching these dangerous creatures with his bare hands. The story goes that this chap has been bitten so many times that the virus no longer has any effect on him. Even that most poisonous of all reptiles, the Gila monster, has no terrors for him. He swims along the shore where venomous reptiles most abound, and fearlessly attacks any and all that promise any income to his employer.

In a very rare book by General Sir Arthur Thurlow Cunynghame, entitled, *My Command in South Africa*, 1880, I find the following:

The subject of snake bites is one of no small interest in this country.

Liquid ammonia is, *par excellence*, the best antidote. It must be administered immediately after the bite, both externally, and internally, in its concentrated form.

The 'Eau de luce' and other nostrums sold for this purpose have ammonia for their main ingredient. But it generally happens in the case of a snake bite that the remedy is not at hand, and hours may elapse before it can be obtained. In this case the following treatment will work well. Tie a ligature *above* the bite, scarify the wound deeply with a knife, and allow it to bleed freely. After having drawn an ounce of blood, remove the ligature and ignite three times successively about two drams of gunpowder right on the wound.

If gunpowder be not at hand, an ordinary fuse will answer the purpose: or, in default of this, the glowing end of a piece of wood from the fire. Having done this, proceed to administer as much brandy as the patient will take. Intoxicate him as rapidly as possible, and, once intoxicated, he is safe. If, however, through delay in treatment, the poison has once got into circulation no amount of brandy will either intoxicate him or save his life.

An odd character, rejoicing in the nick-name of Jack the Viper, is mentioned on page 763 of Hone's *Table Book*, 1829. In part the writer says:

Jack has traveled, seen the world, and profited by his travels; for he has learned to be contented. He is not entirely idle, nor wholly industrious. If he can get a crust sufficient for the day, he leaves the evil of it should visit him. The first time I saw him was in the high noon of a scorching day, at an inn in Laytonstone. He came in while a sudden storm descended, and a rainbow of exquisite majesty vaulted the earth. Sitting down at a table, he beckoned the hostess for his beer, and conversed freely with his acquaintance. By his arch replies I found that I was in company with an original – a man that might stretch forth his arms in the wilderness without fear, and like Paul, grasp an adder without harm. He playfully entwined his fingers with their coils and curled crests, and played with their forked tongues. He had unbuttoned his waistcoat, and as cleverly as a fish woman handles her eels, let out several snakes and adders, warmed by his breast, and spread them on the table. He took off his hat, and others of different sizes and lengths twisted before me; some of them, when he unbuttoned his shirt, returned to the genial temperature of his skin; and some curled around the legs of the table, and others rose in a defensive attitude. He irritated and humored them, to express either pleasure or pain at his will.

Some were purchased by individuals, and Jack pocketed his gains, observing, 'A frog, or a mouse, occasionally, is enough for a snake's satisfaction.'

The Naturalist's Cabinet says, that,

> In presence of the Grand Duke of Tuscany, while the philosophers were making elaborate dissertations on the danger of the poison of vipers, taken inwardly, a viper catcher, who happened to be present, requested that a quantity of it might be put into a vessel; and then, with the utmost confidence, and to the astonishment of the whole company, he drank it off. Everyone expected the man instantly to drop down dead; but they soon perceived their mistake, and found that, taken inwardly, the poison was as harmless as water.

William Oliver, a viper catcher at Bath, was the first who discovered that, by the application of olive oil, the bite of the viper is effectually cured. On the first of June, 1735, he suffered himself to be bitten by an old black viper; and after enduring the agonizing symptoms of approaching death, by using olive oil he perfectly recovered.

Vipers' flesh was formerly esteemed for its medicinal virtues, and its salt was thought to exceed every other animal product in giving vigor to a languid constitution. According to Cornelius Heinrich Agrippa (called Agrippa of Nettesheim), a German philosopher, and student of alchemy and magic, who was born in 1486, and died in 1535, 'if you would handle adders and snakes without harm, wash your hands in the juice of radishes, and you may do so without harm.'

Even though it may seem a digression, I yield to the temptation to include here an extraordinary 'snake story' taken from *An Actor Abroad*, which Edmund Leathes published in 1880:

I will here relate the story of a sad death – I might feel inclined to call it suicide – which occurred in Melbourne shortly before my arrival in the colonies. About a year previous to the time of which I am now writing, a gentleman of birth and education, a Cambridge B.A., a barrister by profession and a literary man by choice, with his wife and three children emigrated to Victoria. He arrived in Melbourne with one hundred and fifty pounds in his pocket, and hope unlimited in his heart.

Poor man! He, like many another man, quickly discovered that muscles in Australia are more marketable than brains. His little store of money began to melt under the necessities of his wife and family. To make matters worse he was visited by a severe illness. He was confined to his bed for some weeks, and during his convalescence his wife presented him with another of those 'blessings to the poor man', a son.

It was Christmas time, his health was thoroughly restored, he naturally possessed a vigorous constitution; but his heart was beginning to fail him, and his funds were sinking lower and lower.

At last one day, returning from a long and solitary walk, he sat down with pen and paper and made a calculation by which he found he had sufficient money left to pay the insurance upon his life for one year, which, in the case of his death occurring within that time, would bring to his widow the sum of three thousand pounds. He went to the insurance office, and made his application – was examined by the doctor – the policy was made out, his life was insured. From that day he grew moody and morose, despair had conquered hope.

At this time a snake-charmer came to Melbourne, who advertised a wonderful cure for snakebites. This charmer took one of the halls in the town, and there displayed his live stock, which consisted of a great number of the most deadly and venomous snakes which were to be found in India and Australia.

This man had certainly some most wonderful antidote to the poison of a snake's fangs. In his exhibitions he would allow a cobra to bite a dog or a rabbit, and, in a short time after he had applied his nostrum the animal would thoroughly revive; he advertised his desire to perform upon humanity, but, of course, he could find no one who would be fool enough to risk his life so unnecessarily.

The advertisement caught the eye of the unfortunate emigrant, who at once proceeded to the hall where the snake charmer was holding his exhibition. He offered himself to be experimented upon; the fanatic snake-charmer was delighted, and an appointment was made for the same evening as soon as the 'show' should be over.

The evening came; the unfortunate man kept his appointment, and, in the presence of several witnesses, who tried to dissuade him from the trial, bared his arm and placed it in the cage of an enraged cobra and was quickly bitten. The nostrum was applied apparently in the same manner as it had been to the lower animals which had that evening been experimented upon, but whether it was that the poor fellow wilfully did something to prevent its taking effect – or whatever the reason – he soon became insensible, and in a couple of hours he was taken home to his wife and family – a corpse. The next morning the snake-charmer had flown, and left his snakes behind him.

The insurance company at first refused payment of the policy, asserting that the death was suicide; the case was tried and the company lost it, and the widow received the three thousand pounds. The snake charmer was sought in vain; he had the good fortune and good sense to be seen no more in the Australian colonies.

As several methods of combating the effects of poisons have been mentioned in the foregoing pages, I feel in duty bound to carry the subject a little farther and present a list of antidotes.

I shall not attempt to educate my readers in the art of medicine, but simply to give a list of such ordinary materials as are to be found in practically every household, materials cited as antidotes for the more common poisons. I have taken them from the best authorities obtainable and they are offered in the way of first aid, to keep the patient alive till the doctor arrives; and if they should do no good, they can hardly do harm.

The first great rule to be adopted is *send for the doctor at once* and give him all possible information about the case without delay. Use every possible means to keep the patient at a normal temperature. When artificial respiration is necessary, always get hold of the tongue and pull it well forward in order to keep the throat clear, then turn the patient over on his face and press the abdomen to force out the air, then turn him over on the back so that the lungs may fill again, repeating this again and again till the doctor arrives. The best stimulants are strong tea or coffee; but when these are not sufficient, a tablespoon of brandy, whisky, or wine may be added.

Vegetable and mineral poisons, with few exceptions, act as efficiently in the blood as in the stomach. Animal poisons act only through the blood, and are inert when introduced into the stomach. Therefore there is absolutely no danger in sucking the virus from a snake bite, except that the virus should not be allowed to touch any spot where the skin is broken.

Notes

1. Infamous case of a chorus girl, Susan Geary, whose body was found in Boston Harbour in 1905. A Dr McLeod, allegedly part of a band of malpractitioners, was convicted of causing her death through performing a botched abortion.
2. Signor Blitz was an English magician and ventriloquist who moved to America in 1834.
3. Charles Bertram, a British magician renowned for this catch phrase.

Biographical note

Harry Houdini was born Erik Weisz in Budapest, Hungary in 1874. The son of a rabbi, Houdini had five siblings, along with whom he emigrated to the USA in 1878. After living for a couple of years in Appleton, Wisconsin, Houdini's family moved to New York City in 1880.

Beginning his career as a nine-year-old trapeze artist, Houdini styled himself, 'Ehrich, the prince of the air', showing a trend for renaming himself that was to continue as he later took on the name 'Houdini', a tribute to the French magician Jean-Eugène Robert-Houdin.

Originally performing as part of a double act with his brother 'Dash', Houdini teamed up in 1893 with his newly married wife, Wilhelmina Beatrice Rahner; she would remain his stage assistant for the rest of his career. Houdini's handcuff acts soon became Vaudeville hits and, in 1900, his manager arranged a tour of Europe, where he rapidly became a sensation.

Returning to the United States, Houdini further developed his act, centring it around escapes rather than handcuffs. The feats that he accomplished remain legendary to this day: escaping from a water-filled milk can, the Chinese water torture cell, the suspended straitjackets and even the stomach of a whale.

In 1923, Houdini became President of the Society of American Magicians. However, Houdini's achievements and interests were not confined to magic. He was a keen pioneer aviator and in 1910 he achieved the first powered flight over Australia. Houdini's foray into acting also led him to set up his own production company 'The Film Development Corporation'.

Houdini died of peritonitis as the result of a ruptured appendix in 1926, having collapsed during a show at the Garrick Theatre in Detroit.